PRAYER

101

PRAYER 101

WHAT IT IS
•
WHAT IT ISN'T
•
HOW TO DO IT

DON M. AYCOCK

BROADMAN
&HOLMAN
PUBLISHERS
Nashville, Tennessee

© 1998
by Don M. Aycock
All rights reserved
Printed in the United States of America

0–8054–1500–9

Published by Broadman & Holman Publishers, Nashville, Tennessee
Acquisitions & Development Editor: Leonard G. Goss
Typesetting: PerfecType

Dewey Decimal Classification: 248.3
Subject Heading: Prayer
Library of Congress Card Catalog Number: 98–11175

Library of Congress Cataloging-in-Publication Data
Aycock, Don M.
    Prayer 101: what it is, what it isn't, how to do it / Don M. Aycock.
        p. cm.
    Includes bibliographical references.
    ISBN 0–8054–1500–9
    1. Prayer--Christianity
    I. Title.
    BV210.2.A89   1998
    248.3'2—dc21

                                                        98–11175
                                                        CIP

1 2 3 4 5 02 01 00 99 98

Dedication

This book is dedicated to three of the best people in the world—my wife, Carla, and our teenage sons, Chris and Ryan. I'm not the least bit prejudiced in calling them the best. Carla is my prayer partner of nearly a quarter of a century, and having teenagers will improve your prayer life greatly!

And to the saints of the McLean Baptist Church in Memphis, Tennessee. Way to go, guys!

Contents

Introduction

Chapter One
A Stubborn Misunderstanding of Prayer   6

Chapter Two
You Are Invited to Pray   20

Chapter Three
Pray Like This   34

Chapter Four
Your Attitude Is Important   46

Chapter Five
Others Need Your Prayers   60

Chapter Six
Honesty in Prayer   72

Chapter Seven
God Will Strengthen You Through Prayer   90

Chapter Eight
Prayer and God's Will for Your Life   104

Introduction

The ancient Roman word *precarious* originally meant "obtained by prayer or begging." Today something that is dependent on anything uncertain is called precarious. That is what some people think prayer is—a last resort, a beggar's choice, a weakling's fallback. For all of the misunderstandings and even deliberate attacks on prayer, one fact is certain—people pray. A recent Gallup poll reveals that over 75 percent of Americans pray.[1] That is an astounding number considering that less than 25 percent of Americans regularly attend worship services. Regardless of their outward religiosity, people still reach out to God in prayer. They want some contact with Truth and to know that life makes some sort of sense.

Blaise Pascal, the seventeenth-century mathematician and philosopher, was right. He wrote, "The heart has its reasons, of which reason knows nothing;

1

we feel it in many things." We may not be able to give an adequate explanation for our urges to pray, but our "heart has its reasons." We *feel* it is the right thing to do. That feeling, that urge to reach out beyond ourselves, is God given. We might call it a "homing" instinct. It is what helps you want to read this book and do something about it.

I will not be spending much time in this book defending prayer. Other books do that. What I will be doing is walking with you, much like a guide on a tour, as we move through this country called "prayer." Like a group of tourists, we will concentrate on seeing the highlights and will not linger very long in any one place. We will look first at what prayer is *not*. By learning what it is not, we will be in a better position to learn what it *is*. Then we will examine several key passages of Scripture and open them up to discover what prayer does to us and to those around us. Please read all of the Scripture passages that are suggested throughout this book. They will prepare you to better understand the discussion in each chapter.

The "bottom line" for many people regarding prayer is this: They want to know, "Can prayer actually *do* something to make my life different and better?" We will be exploring this question in different ways in the pages that follow. Right now, though, I want to give you a personal illustration of what prayer can do for us.

Several years ago I was offered a new position with the Baptist Brotherhood Commission to help develop and launch Men's Ministries. Working with men and developing resources for that work interested me greatly. Taking that job would require moving my family several hundred miles from where we lived, transferring my sons to a new school, and having my wife find a new teaching position. We prayed intensely about the matter for several weeks. The day came for me to fly from my home in Louisiana to Memphis, Tennessee, to formally interview for the job. As I waited in the airport for the plane, I continued praying. An unusually strong sense of peace and wellbeing came over me. I recorded my feelings in a notebook. This is what I felt and wrote:

I have a great sense of well-being now. I'm waiting for a flight to Memphis. This feeling is much more than *events*—like the new job at the Brotherhood Commission. It is more related to my sense that life, with all its craziness, makes sense. We try *so* hard and work ourselves to death, but for what? It's OK to be shy, unsure, ungraceful, or anything else. Simply to *be*—that is the goal!

Praying did not make my life "easier" in that it took away the need to make decisions or problems that cropped up. What prayer did was to give the divine "Yes" to my life (see 2 Cor. 1:19). Circumstances changed, and after two and a half years of working with men I was offered another position in Memphis. Prayer again helped me to make a decision to accept the position and begin a new chapter in my ministry.

I do not write as an expert on prayer. I am a struggling pilgrim just like you are. My journey has included serving as a pastor for twenty years, a writer for longer than that, and an employee for a national denominational ministry. This last assignment has allowed me to travel across the country and get to know many people. I have discovered that people everywhere are struggling and working to know what God wants and to carry it out.

Yes, prayer matters. It *does* something. Now let us examine just what it does.

Read Matthew 6:5–8

"But you, when you pray, go into your inner room, close your door and pray to your Father who is in secret, and your Father who sees what is done in secret will reward you."

Matthew 6:6

1
A Stubborn Misunderstanding
of Prayer

WHAT DOES THE WORD *prayer* bring to your mind? A regular meeting at church? A last-ditch effort to stave off some disaster? An intimate communication between you and God? All of these images, or others, might come to mind when we think of prayer.

A ball game is about to begin. Silence is called for and someone begins to intone words of protection for the players. Is that prayer? A soldier in a battle raises his eyes to heaven in a silent plea for protection. Is that prayer? A woman kneels on a bench in a church building and begins to commune with God in a way that seems more like a dialogue than a monologue. Is that prayer? A young person faces an important test, so she fingers the cross hanging around her neck. Is that prayer? As is obvious by just these few images, prayer has many facets.

George Appleton writes:
The word "prayer" embraces a number of
meanings and covers a number of activities.
In its most elementary form it is asking God
for the things we need, material or spiritual.
It can be thanksgiving for what God has
done for us; it can be worship of God for
what he is. It can be fellowship with God,
enjoying our touch with him, quiet reflec-
tion in his presence. It can be the expression
of our concern for people or for what is hap-
pening in the world and in the Church. It
can be vocal, when we express ourselves in
words, or it can be silent and contemplative,
resting in his presence, the sphere of the
timeless and the eternal. Prayer is as essential to the inner life as breath is to the body.[1]

Prayer, as we see above, can be many things and
comes in many forms. But not all ideas about prayer
are biblically correct. We will be considering many
ideas about prayer in this small book. But sometimes
we can tell what something is by discovering what it is
not. This is true with prayer. If, at the very beginning
of our study, we raise several popular ideas that are
probably wrong, then we will be on our way toward
discovering what prayer really is. Let me point out
something here, though. These incorrect ideas about
prayer are stubborn, and they keep cropping up in
every generation. Since they are immature notions,
new Christians are especially prone to believe them.

When Christians have a chance to grow and mature in relationship to Christ, prayer will often take on a deeper meaning.

Prayer Is Not a Lottery

A lottery is a game of chance. A person gambles, hoping that what he bets will pay off more than the original bet. I do not mean to sound crass when I suggest that some people seem to think of prayer as a lottery. They think, "Hey, I'll say a prayer in this situation. It couldn't hurt anything, and it might pay off big."

This way of thinking is purely selfish. The sole motive behind the act is to gamble that a few words mumbled to the deity might "do some good." As you read the Bible, you will find many prayers addressed to God. Many of those are said by people who were in trouble. They asked for help. The difference between those prayers and the contemporary prayer-as-lottery view is this: the people in the Bible who prayed for help already had an established relationship with God. They were asking the help of the one whom they knew as the Lord. They were not just casting out verbiage in the hope that it might possibly be heard by "the man upstairs" and answered affirmatively.

Prayer Is Not a Twist of God's Arm

Another popular notion about prayer is that it is a way to make God do something he does not want to do. It is a way to twist God's arm to force him to do your will. Most people would never state the case so boldly and probably would even deny that is what they believe. However, when you hear what some people pray for and the way they ask for it, you realize that they are trying to force their wills upon God.

But doesn't the Bible have examples of this kind of prayer? Aren't some situations in the Bible exactly that? Consider the example of Jesus cursing the fig tree. On what we call Palm Sunday, Jesus entered Jerusalem and then returned to Bethany to spend the night. The next morning, when Jesus and the disciples were on their way back to Jerusalem, Jesus spotted a fig tree in full leaf. He went up to the tree, expecting to find it as full of fruit as it was full of green leaves. He found no fruit, however. Mark 11:14 states, "Then he said to the tree, 'May no one ever eat fruit from you again.' And his disciples heard him say it" (NIV).The next day, Tuesday morning, Jesus and the twelve were again going to Jerusalem. They saw that the tree had withered overnight. Simon Peter said, "Rabbi, look! The fig tree you cursed has withered!" (v. 21 NIV).

This story causes some modern people trouble because they misunderstand the concept of curse in the Bible. A curse was not what we today would call a "four-letter word." It was not a "nasty" reference. A good Oriental curse was earthy, specific, and a call to action. It may have sounded something like: "May the fleas of a thousand camels infest your armpits," or

"May all your teeth fall out but one, and in that one may you get a toothache." In cursing the fig tree, Jesus was calling for action on the part of his disciples and using it as an object lesson or a prophetic symbolism.

This story of the fig tree is connected by Mark with the cleansing of the temple. A fig tree with no fruit was exactly like a temple that produced no fruit. The cursing of the tree was a prophetic sign. The fig tree's leaves promised fruit, but they bore no fruit. The tree's appearance was deceptive. It was a symbol of what Jesus had found in the temple. It, too, looked promising. The temple had a long history and promised seekers that they could find a place of worship, a place that would help them find God. What they found was chaos like the day after Christmas at Wal-Mart. To this farce Jesus raised his whip and his voice and said in effect, "Enough! You shall not make my Father's house a place of empty promises in which you are more interested in revenue than reverence."

Jesus' action was in line with the Old Testament prophets. He saw the leaders of the temple as being like the one described by Jeremiah: "'I will surely snatch them away,' declares the LORD; 'There will be no grapes on the vine and no figs on the fig tree, and the leaf will wither; and what I have given them will pass away'" (Jer. 8:13). Bible scholar Richard Gardner notes that this action is symbolic. He writes, "Jesus' action, then, signifies the judgment of God on a religious community that 'is covered with the ostentatious foliage of external piety,' but in which 'truly

obedient deeds, the fruit of religion, are lacking. . .'"[2]
Jesus, quoting from Isaiah 56:7 and Jeremiah 7:11,
said, "'My house will be called a house of prayer for all
nations,' but you have made it 'a den of robbers'"
(Mark 11:17 NIV).

You see, Jesus called for action with his curse.
This curse may have been a form of prayer in that
Jesus used it to accomplish God's will. He was not
simply being spiteful; nor was he lashing out from hurt
pride. Jesus did not try to make the Father do something he was unwilling to do. Jesus worked in harmony with the will of the Father and not against it.[3]
Working in harmony with the will of God is central
when we think about prayer. We pray to lay hold of
God's willingness, not to make God do our will.

Prayer Is Not an Automatic Guarantee of Success

A subtle misunderstanding of prayer is to think
of it as a guarantee of success. Someone might think,
"I really need to get an edge. I'll ask God to help me
win." Now we certainly want to pray in all things, but
to imagine that prayer will give us a guarantee of success is immature. So how do we pray for things like
our jobs and decisions we need to make? What good
does prayer do in these situations? Consider the example of John Marks Templeton.

Templeton is the founder of the successful Templeton group of mutual funds. He is regarded as one of
Wall Street's wisest investors. Many years ago he

committed himself to Christ and became a man of prayer. He began to open all of the directors' and shareholders' meetings with prayer. But he points out that prayer is never used as a tool in making specific stock selections. Templeton notes, "That would be a gross misinterpretation of God's methods. What we do pray for is wisdom. We pray that the decisions we make today will be wise decisions and that our talks about different stocks will be wise talks. Of course, our discussions and decisions are fallible and sometimes flawed. No one should expect that, just because he begins with prayer, every decision he makes is going to be profitable."[4] He continues, "However, I do believe that, if you pray, you will make fewer stupid mistakes."

Prayer is no substitute for hard work and personal responsibility. It helps us make decisions and work smarter, but it is not an automatic guarantee of success.

Prayer Is Not Meaningless Ritual

My family has prayer at mealtime. My wife and I have prayed at mealtime since we first married, and we have taught our children to say grace at the table. This ritual is important to us, and it expresses our daily gratitude for our food. Many people say a prayer at mealtime, or before bed, or at a ball game. The saying of the prayers might be meaningful, or it might just be a ritual performed at stated times simply because they have always done it.

We need to remember that such rituals can be important, but they might seem strange to those who do not understand them. During the early days of our nation, a traveling preacher went to a frontier town to hold religious services. The town had received very little religious influence before the preacher's arrival. While he was there, he stayed with a family in town who had a little boy. On the first evening of his arrival everyone gathered around the table for supper. The preacher bowed his head and said an audible prayer. The little boy had never seen anything like that before. The child saw the preacher on the street the next day and asked, "Are you the fellow who talks to his plate?"[5]

Prayer Is Not a Purely Personal Religious Act with No Social Consequences

Praying is one of the most intimate things a person can do. To reach out to the God of creation with words and feelings is a tremendously personal act. In fact some people have described religion in general and prayer in particular with reference to this privacy. I have read definitions such as, "Religion is what one does with his solitude." I am not sure what that means because we can do many things with our solitude. Such a definition tries to paint religion and prayer as nothing more than a purely private communication between a person and God.

The problem with that definition is that it stops too soon. Prayer is personal and intimate, but it is not purely private. One of the overwhelming teachings about prayer in the Bible is that prayer moves us from our selfish preoccupations to something beyond ourselves. The book of James in the New Testament states: "What good is it, my brothers, if a man claims to have faith but has no deeds? Can such faith save him? Suppose a brother or sister is without clothes and daily food. If one of you says to him, 'Go, I wish you well; keep warm and well fed,' but does nothing about his physical needs, what good is it? In the same way, faith by itself, if it is not accompanied by action, is dead" (2:14–17 NIV).

Prayer, in other words, should move us not only toward God, but toward our fellow humans. Frederick Douglass was a slave who narrated his life in a book that was first published in 1845. He told of the conditions under which he lived. Consider one section from his autobiography:

There were four slaves of us in the kitchen— my sister Eliza, my aunt Priscilla, Henry, and myself; and we were allowed less than a half a bushel of corn-meal per week, and very little else, either in the shape of meat or vegetables. It was not enough for us to subsist upon. We were therefore reduced to the wretched necessity of living at the expense of our neighbors. This we did by begging and stealing, whichever came handy in the time of need, the one being considered as legitimate as the other. A great many times have we poor creatures been nearly perishing with hunger, when food in abundance lay

smouldering in the safe and smoke-house,
and our pious mistress was aware of the fact;
and yet that mistress and her husband would
kneel every morning, and pray that God
would bless them in basket and store![6]

How does that stack up against the instruction of James?

How many people will go to bed hungry tonight while praying for something to eat tomorrow? Are their efforts just empty words poured out into an uncaring universe?

Prayer Is Not Getting in Touch with Mystical Powers

We live in an age of generic spirituality when we often hear about spiritual values. To many people, spiritual values refer to inner personal values rather than to God. A term that is often associated with spirituality today is "New Age." That is something of a catch-all term that lumps all religious, metaphysical, and spiritual quests into the same category. It might include channeling, tarot cards, belief in reincarnation, and other such manifestations. I have noticed that some people use any talk of religious values to include even the major religions such as Judaism and Christianity.

So what is prayer in New Age philosophy? It is the attempt to get in touch with the mystical forces of the universe and to influence those forces. That is done through repeating a mantra—a special word or phrase—or by deeply meditating. The attempt to influence the powers of the universe traditionally has been called magic.

C. S. Lewis, a well-known writer from England, was especially careful not to allow his prayers to sink to the level of seeming to be magic. He wrote, "The very question 'Does prayer work?' puts us in the wrong frame of mind from the outset. 'Work': as if it were magic, or a machine—something that functions automatically."[7] His point is that prayer is communication between God and humans, not a scientific formula in which everything is certain. Nor is prayer an "open sesame" guaranteed to open the doors of heaven. Again, that concept is magic.

Magic is defined as: "1. The art that purports to control or forecast natural events, effects, or forces by invoking the supernatural. 2. The practice of using charms, spells, or rituals to attempt to produce supernatural effects or to control events in nature."[8]

Christian prayer is different from magic because it seeks to get in touch with, not a what, but a whom. In other words, prayer reaches out to God as a loving Heavenly Father who wants the best for his children rather than to a mysterious, capricious force of nature. Prayer is thus personal communication that moves beyond the "gimme" aspect of life to communion with the Holy God. One person wrote, "The big watershed is moving from trying to control God to letting God direct me."[9]

Learn to avoid some of the stubborn misunderstandings about prayer. Learn to pray. It will change your life.

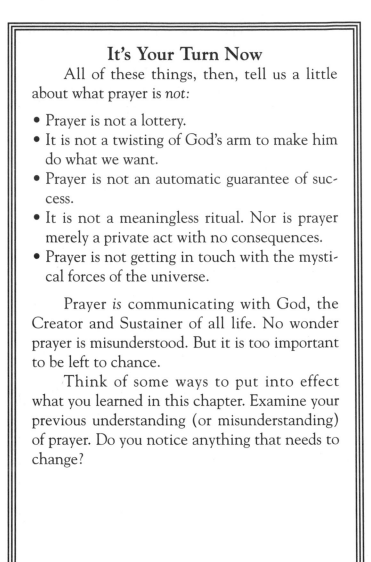

It's Your Turn Now

All of these things, then, tell us a little about what prayer is *not:*

- Prayer is not a lottery.
- It is not a twisting of God's arm to make him do what we want.
- Prayer is not an automatic guarantee of success.
- It is not a meaningless ritual. Nor is prayer merely a private act with no consequences.
- Prayer is not getting in touch with the mystical forces of the universe.

Prayer *is* communicating with God, the Creator and Sustainer of all life. No wonder prayer is misunderstood. But it is too important to be left to chance.

Think of some ways to put into effect what you learned in this chapter. Examine your previous understanding (or misunderstanding) of prayer. Do you notice anything that needs to change?

Questions for Reflection and Discussion

1. What do you usually think of when you hear the word *prayer*?

2. Can you list other things or ideas that prayer is *not*?

3. Can prayer be a guarantee of success in any endeavor?

4. What are some ways that people try to make God do what they want him to do?

5. What are some of the social consequences that might be associated with prayer?

6. What is prayer in New Age religious expressions?

7. What is the most important insight you learned from this chapter?

> ## *Read Luke 11:1–13*
>
> "For everyone who asks, receives; and he who seeks, finds; and to him who knocks, it will be opened."
>
> Luke 11:10

2
You Are Invited
To Pray

"DEAR FRIEND, You are cordially invited to attend a meeting between you and God. The time is flexible, and you may accept this invitation anytime you want. Your Host is awaiting your reply. Please do not delay."

If this invitation arrived in your mailbox, how would you respond? My first response would be to check the postmark! Aside from that, we might wonder who would send such an invitation. Imagine it—an invitation from God himself.

The fact is that God has actually given us an invitation like that. The whole concept of prayer is based on this one fact: *God wants to have communication with us.* That overriding fact needs to be kept in mind as we think about prayer. To pray is to risk. The acclaimed author of *Roots*, Alex Haley, once said about taking risks, "Nothing is more important. Too often we are taught how *not* to take risks. When we are children in school, for example, we are told to respect our heroes, our founders, the great people of the past. We are directed to their portraits hanging on walls and in hallways and reproduced in textbooks. What we are not told is that these leaders, who look so serene and secure in those portraits, were in fact rule-*breakers*. They were risk-takers in the best sense of the word; they dared to be different."[1] Be a risk-taker. Learn to pray.

A Normal Request

"One of His disciples said to Him, 'Lord, teach us to pray.'" From that simple request came Jesus' teaching on prayer. The disciple, who is unnamed here, had noticed that Jesus' life was characterized by prayer. He wanted the Lord to pass on to him and the other disciples his teachings about prayer. Religious guides and rabbis of that day taught their followers how to pray. The disciple knew this because his request included the words, "as John also taught his disciples."

This is the beginning point of genuine prayer—a desire to reach out to God. The real quest of prayer is to know God, not to get stuff. How different this is from the "name-it-and-claim-it" mentality that sees religious faith as a fast lane to riches! Prayer is interpersonal communication between a person and God. All of the open intimacy implied in communication is present. This includes everything from humor to anger, from request to praise. In prayer we can talk to

God as we address another person. When I was a child, for example, I used to tell God jokes. (Then someone spoiled this for me and pointed out that he already knew the punch line.)

Jesus demonstrated the ongoing habit of prayer in his life. His disciples watched him closely and observed the rhythms of his life. At times Jesus was with the public, teaching and healing. At other times he withdrew into solitude with his Father. Apparently the disciples wanted Jesus to teach them a form of words they could use or a pattern of the sort of prayer God hears. They realized the difference between saying prayers, which they did, and actively praying, which they did not do. The former is saying words. The latter is communicating with the heavenly Father in dialogue.

The observance of Jesus' habit of prayer caused the disciples to ask for guidance in their prayer lives. A good habit observed by others can be helpful to them. A person who is seen going to church each week, for example, might help to motivate others to attend. If someone is known as a praying person, others might call on that person for help and guidance. We do not want to flaunt our religious life, however. Jesus told a parable about a Pharisee and a tax gatherer to demonstrate this fact (see Luke 18:9–14). We may, however, ask God to teach us to pray.

Why spend our time and effort in prayer? What is the purpose of prayer? Donald Bloesch, a theologian, has answered this question succinctly. He writes,

"The ultimate goal of the life of prayer is the glorification of God and the advancement of his kingdom. Indeed, kingdom service is precisely what gives glory to God. To pray that the glory of God might be made manifest among people in the world is to pray for the fulfillment of God's highest will. It means to pray for the dawning of a new age, when all people may come to know the reality and sovereignty of God (Isa. 66:18; Phil. 2:10, 11; 1 Pet. 4:11)."[2] Our prayers are part of the means by which God's rule spreads throughout the world.

Prayer and Persistence

The following question is often raised: "Why doesn't God answer our prayers?" Jesus knew this question, too. In teaching his disciples to pray he addressed the issue of unanswered prayer by telling a parable about a friend who awakened a neighbor in the middle of the night in order to get provisions for a traveler. Hospitality was considered a sacred duty in that era.

The setting of this parable is small village life in Jesus' time. Common people slept in small, one-room houses. The family slept on a raised platform and the domestic animals slept on the bare earthen floor. When a family and livestock were bedded down for the night, no one could get up easily without disturbing everyone. That explains the man's reluctance to get up at midnight: "Do not bother me; the door has already been shut and my children and I are in bed; I cannot get up and give you anything" (Luke 11:7).

Even so, his friend continues to knock until the man gets up and lends him three loaves. Jesus made his point in verse 8: "I tell you, even though he will not get up and give him anything because he is his friend, yet because of his persistence he will get up and give him as much as he needs." The word *persistence* is the key. In the original Greek, persistence meant shamelessness. The friend outside had put his duty to his traveling guest above his own need to act "normal." His act was shameless. Even so, he felt compelled to act.

In this parable Jesus taught about prayer. If an ordinary man can be moved by persistence, then Almighty God can also be moved by it. One person has said, "We must not play at prayer, but must show persistence if we do not receive the answer immediately. It is not that God is unwilling and must be pressed into answering," but rather, "if we do not want what we are asking for enough to be persistent, we do not want it very much. It is not such tepid prayer that is answered."[3] People who pray persistently show they have accepted God's invitation to a lifestyle of prayer.

Without persistence we would live as those whom Theodore Roosevelt described as being "in the gray twilight that knows not victory or defeat."[4]

Ask, Seek, Knock

How would you like a money-saving special on prayer? Ridiculous, you say! I actually saw one in a local paper a few years ago. A person calling herself Sister Roberts placed a quarter-page ad in a newspaper. That ad read in part: "The Southern Born Spiritualist who brings you the solutions to the mysteries of the Deep South, seeks to help many thousands of people who have been Crossed, Have Spells, Can't Hold Money, Want Luck. . . . If you are seeking a sure-fire woman to Aid in Peace, Love and Prosperity in the home, you need to see this woman of God today!" After pointing out how close to God she was, the lady closed with these words in big bold type: "Special This Week: All readings only $5.00 each."

When Jesus said, "Ask . . . seek . . . knock" (v. 9), did he mean anything like that? Are we "guaranteed" anything beyond God's care? A look at the original words in this text will help us answer these questions. The words *ask*, *seek*, and *knock* in the Greek language are present imperatives. A present imperative is a command to continuous action. Jesus thus said to the disciples, "Keep on asking, keep on seeking, keep on knocking."[5] One quick prayer ripped off in a moment of need may or may not be answered. Jesus' point is that we can be assured of God's answer as we continue to seek God's will. Some answers come only after much effort and patience.

We have many needs because life is so unpredictable. This notice appeared in the window of a coat store in Nottingham, England: "We have been established for over 100 years and been pleasing and displeasing customers ever since. We have made money and lost money, suffered the effects of coal nationalization, coal rationing, government control, and bad payers. We have been cussed and discussed, messed about, lied to, held up, robbed, and swindled. The only reason we stay in business is to see what happens next."

I can relate to that. Can you? We are wholly right in asking for God's guidance, help, and protection. Some things cannot be planned or avoided in advance. Gracie Allen, the late wife of George Burns, once received a small, live alligator as a gag. She did not know what else to do with it, so she put it in the bathtub and left for an appointment. When Gracie returned she found this note from her maid: "Dear Miss Allen: Sorry, but I have quit. I don't work in houses where there is an alligator. I'd have told you this when I took on, but I never thought it would come up."

A question might be put to all persons who pray: "What do you want and how badly do you want it?" Verses 9 and 10 suggest that those who want God and will persist until they know God will eventually succeed. God invites us to a lifestyle of prayer where we will continually ask, seek, and knock. Continuity keeps prayer in the realm of a personal relationship. This is quite different from thinking of prayer as a celestial candy machine in which we drop in a prayer and out pops the prize.

Look carefully at verse 10. Jesus said, "For everyone who asks, receives; and he who seeks, finds; and to him who knocks, it will be opened." People who develop a lifelong habit of prayer find that they move closer and closer to what God intends for them. They seek God's will, not their own. They ask for God's goals, not for merely selfish goals. They knock in order to receive what is best for them in the long run, not the short term. One commentator has noted about verse 10, "God does not have to be waked or cajoled into giving us what we need—many gifts he bestows on the ungodly and ungrateful; but his choicest blessings are reserved for those who will value them and who show their appreciation by asking until they receive."[6]

A story is told about the ancient Greek philosopher Socrates. A young man went to him and said, "Be my teacher. I want to learn everything you know." Socrates took the young man down to the Mediterranean Sea and pushed him under the water and held him a while. When he pulled him up Socrates asked the young man, "What do you want?" The man said, "I want to learn." The teacher pushed him under again, held him longer, and again asked what he wanted. His answer still was, "I want to learn." Finally Socrates held him under for a long while. Once again he pulled him up and asked, "What do you want?" The young man shouted, "I want air!" The philosopher said, "When you want learning as much as you want air, then you will be ready to study with me."

God desires that we be hungry to learn from him and to know him personally. This takes both time and effort. God invites us to pray, but he will not make us pray. When we are hungry to know him, we will find him.

Getting Good Gifts

"Something good is going to happen to you today!" Does that sound familiar? A televangelist used to say that each time he was on the air. His motto was vaguely biblical. Jesus did promise blessings for his followers, though the followers might not even be aware of the blessings. Even so, God can be trusted to do what is necessary for his people.

Jesus posed an "if-then" situation to illustrate God's ongoing care for his creation. If a child would ask his father for a fish, what cruel father would give the child a snake instead? If a hungry youngster wanted an egg, would any father hand him a scorpion? The implied answer to these questions is "No!"

I am the father of twin boys who are now teenagers. I take great pains to make sure my boys are fed, clothed, housed, educated, and loved. If a normal man like me would take such great care of his sons, can we not believe that God would take even better care of his children? Luke 11:13 reads, "If you then, being evil, know how to give good gifts to your children, how much more will your heavenly Father give the Holy Spirit to those who ask Him?"

God's response to our prayers is consistent with his good nature. God loves people and wants the best for them. His gift of the Holy Spirit is evidence that God responds to prayer out of his goodness. Luke indicates that the Holy Spirit is the best gift God could give his children. Christians receive this gift at the time of their salvation.

The Holy Spirit works with us as we pray consistently. The Spirit keeps us from giving up when things are rough. A good example of consistent prayer is Luther Rice, who lived from 1783 until 1836. He was a single man who was appointed as a missionary to India by the American Board of Commissioners for Foreign Missions, an interdenominational group. Rice became a Baptist in 1812 and was denied support. He returned to the United States to raise the funds he and Adoniram and Ann Judson needed. Rice never returned to the mission field in India. Instead he traveled extensively promoting mission causes within the Triennial Convention, the first general association of Baptists in the United States. Luther Rice's life was characterized by persistent prayer. The Spirit of God helped him in his travels and work on behalf of missions. He accepted God's invitation to pray.

Medical doctor and researcher Herbert Benson says that "humans are, in a profound physical way, 'wired for God.'"[7] Benson notes that we come into the world with hard-wired instincts, such as fear of heights and fear of snakes. These are genetically predisposed patterns of behavior. His discovery that humans are "wired for God" came to him suddenly. He said, "My interactions with patients, their families, and with people in general led me to believe that my hypothesis was sound. The idea that humans are wired for God, that we are custom-made to engage in and exercise beliefs, and that spiritual beliefs are the most powerful of that sort, felt like a truth that had always existed inside of me and inside of humankind to which I had suddenly gained conscious access."[8]

Our physically based need to interact with God is powerful. Benson writes, "Religious groups encourage all kinds of health-affirming activities, fellowship and socializing perhaps first among them, but also prayer, volunteerism, familiar rituals, and music. Prayer, in particular, appears to be therapeutic, the specifics of which science will continue to explore."[9] Benson has scientifically affirmed a biblical truth. We have a need to reach out to God. Why? Because he has already reached out to us. That may be the physically based situation that Benson calls being "wired for God."

I experienced this strong need to reach out to God in a striking way when I visited the site of the federal building in Oklahoma City one year after it was bombed. The area is now fenced off. Hundreds of items like messages and toys and plaques are tied onto the fence. More than a hundred other people were there the same time I was. I noticed that nearly everyone was silent. A woman standing next to me had a young daughter who looked to be about four or five years old. The girl kept talking. Finally the mother said, "Honey, you have to be quiet here. This is a sacred place."

What did she mean by that? Why was it sacred? Wasn't it because the enormity of what had happened there brought home our human mortality? Somehow that place reminds people of eternal things. It calls people to consider the deeper issues of life and death. It calls people to pray. You, too, are invited to pray. Will you answer that call? God's invitation to pray is real. RSVP.

It's Your Turn Now

This chapter began with an invitation from the Lord. How will you answer it? Here are several things to consider as you learn to pray.

- You might gather a group and schedule a prayer retreat in which you plan strategies to develop a lifestyle of prayer.
- You might commit yourself to spend a significant amount of time in prayer each week.
- You might choose prayer partners as a way of encouraging each other in your prayer lives.
- You might develop some sort of prayer calendar or journal in which you log your needs, petitions, and answers received.

Questions for Further Reflection and Discussion

1. Do you think the Scripture really gives an invitation to pray?

2. Jesus' first disciples asked, "Lord, teach us to pray." If you could ask Jesus something about prayer, what would it be?

3. Why do you think Jesus made a lifelong habit of prayer?

4. Is there an area of your life for which you need to "ask, seek, and knock?"

5. Recall the story of the philosopher and his would-be disciple. What do you really want out of your relationship with God?

Read Matthew 6:1–15

"Pray, then, in this way. . . ."

Matthew 6:9a

3
Pray Like This

A YOUNG MAN once asked, "Pastor, how should I pray? I've read a book or two on the subject, but I'm still not sure just what it is I'm supposed to do." He was completely serious in his request. The pastor counseled the young man to examine Matthew 6 for guidelines in prayer. It provides a direct teaching selection on prayer from Jesus himself. If anyone can help us learn to pray, he can. The "Lord's Prayer" is Jesus' model for personal prayer.

Getting Our Motives Right

Prayer, like most religious acts, is best done for the benefit of God and his reign and not just for his people. Our prayers are not to be said just so other people will hear us pray and think, "Gee, that person certainly is religious." Prayer is deep personal communication between you and God. When it becomes a show or performance, it ceases to be prayer.

Jesus warned against publicity hunting—doing religiously showy things for people to see. When someone does something for show, the praise he or she gets from other people is the entire reward. There is nothing else. God considers the praises as "paid in full." A former host of a nationally televised religious program stated that the only time she and her husband ever prayed was on television! They never prayed together at home.[1] Prayers said only to be seen by others are not heard by God.

Jesus also warned against wordiness. The pagans, he said, use many words in their prayers. Perhaps they thought that by multiplying words they could somehow make God listen. Jesus knew we cannot force God to do anything. We certainly live in a day of wordiness. Some people use fancy words to say things that could easily be stated more simply, or they try to take the bite out of potentially troubling problems. This evasion of unpleasantness is called *doublespeak*. Consider the following examples:

- A gas company no longer sends a gas bill; now it is called an "energy document."
- An auto company laid off five thousand workers; the company called the layoff a "career alternative enhancement program."
- A recent medical publication warned that jumping off a building could result in "sudden deceleration trauma" upon landing.

- The military no longer says it is going to war; it now engages in "lethal intervention" which could result in "excess mortality."
- Even common devices are subject to becoming other things: a zipper is an "interlocking slide fastener"; a toothbrush is a "home plaque removal instrument."

Prayer is not religious doublespeak. It is deep, committed communication between an individual or groups and God. This fact helps ensure that prayer is offered from the right motives as Jesus taught them.

Getting the Model Right

A friend of mine owns a small mobile home refurbishing business. He once found a crumpled piece of paper in one of the trailers and gave it to me. The handwritten note contains a "formula" for praying. This is what is scrawled on that note:

Get 3 glasses of water at 12 o'clock; pray 3 Our Father prayers, pray 3 23rd Psalms. Set all 3 glasses on refrigerator at 5 A.M. in the morning. Go to front door. Say, "In the name of the Father, in the name of the Son, in the name of the Holy Ghost." Follow Thursday. Follow Friday. Get all bills, place on a white plate; take your right hand and place over bills. Pray like you never prayed before; offer bills each up to God. Set plate on top of refrigerator; lay your Bible on 23rd Psalm; take out as you can pay each bill.

37

Did this formula for prayer work? I guess not. This paper was found in a repossessed trailer!

Jesus did offer a model for his followers to use in praying. It is not some magic formula to success, but it is a guide for us to know what God will listen and respond to. Let us examine the various parts of the Lord's Prayer.

The first two verses pertain to God's rule over people and their honoring him as their Lord.

"Our Father"

Jesus spoke in Aramaic, a language similar to Hebrew. He spoke of God as *Abba,* which is a personal term similar to our term "Daddy." This term expresses our relationship to God and his nature. God is not only the eternal Lord of the universe. He is also the Father of Jesus and of his followers. Someone has noted, "Abba is a term which speaks of God's friendliness and love, as well as of His parental authority; it suggests that the disciples are children who love and trust God and who try to be obedient to Him."[2]

This is a personal term of address. Christians may reach out to God with the realization that he is our heavenly Father who cares for us.

"In heaven"

While the term "Father" suggests that God is close and personal, the term "in heaven" reminds us that God is not just a good buddy next door. He is above and beyond us. God is not earthbound or temporary. He is heavenly and everlasting. He is transcendent.

"Hallowed be Your name"

This part of Jesus' model prayer teaches us that God's name is separate from all other names. It is holy, which is the meaning of the word *hallowed*. In the Bible, someone's name refers to his whole character. God's name is hallowed when his nature and purpose are known and reverenced. People should show reverence for God.

"Your kingdom come"

God's kingdom is his rule in the hearts and lives of his people. To pray this part of the prayer is to pledge yourself to join God's effort to extend his rule to everyone. This prayer is sincere when we want others to know the lordship of God.

"Your will be done, on earth as it is in heaven"

This is a request that God's purpose be carried out among persons. What is his purpose? Fisher Humphreys has written, "God's purpose is to create a worldwide family of persons who freely accept God as their God and who receive his love into their lives, and who respond to him by loving him with all their hearts and loving their neighbors as themselves."[3]

This, in a very succinct manner, is what God wills. When we pray "Your will be done," we are saying, "Lord, I want what you want for me. I pledge to work for your purpose in life."

"Give us this day our daily bread"

God's care for his children includes their total welfare. The needs of the body are important as are the needs of the soul. Jesus taught that God is interested in our everyday needs. This includes food, certainly, but I think it includes all of our basic needs. We may properly pray for *all* matters in our daily lives. These could include our home, our job, our health, our relationships with other people, and our deepest physical and emotional needs. Jesus taught that we can pray about everything that makes up daily life. I take that to mean that God invites our prayers regarding our hurts, our hang-ups, our sexual desires, our loneliness, and anything else we may wish to share with him and ask for his help in. In short, we may rightly pray about everything that touches our lives.

This part of our prayer lives need not be long and cumbersome. A Washington lawyer once got hold of this section of the Model Prayer, and it ended up like this: "We respectively petition, request, and entreat that due and adequate provision be made, this day and the date hereinafter subscribed, for the organizing of such methods of allocation and distribution as may be deemed necessary and proper to assure the reception by and for said petitioners of such quantities of baked cereal products as shall, in the judgment of the aforesaid petitioners, constitute a sufficient supply thereof." I wonder what the whole prayer might look like!

C. S. Lewis pondered the mystery of Jesus' teaching people to pray like this:

> Petitionary prayer is . . . both allowed and commanded to us: "Give us our daily bread." And no doubt it raises a theoretical problem. Can we believe that God ever really modifies His action in response to the suggestions of men? For infinite wisdom does not need telling what is best, and infinite goodness needs no urging to do it. But neither does God need any of those things that are done by his finite agents, whether living or inanimate. He could, if He chose, repair our bodies miraculously without food; or give us food without the aid of farmers, bakers, or butchers; or knowledge without the aid of learned men; or convert the heathen without missionaries. Instead, He allows soils and weather and animals and the muscles, minds, and wills of men to cooperate with His will.[4]

In God's grace, our prayers matter to God! Things happen when people pray. "God," said Pascal, a seventeenth-century philosopher, "instituted prayer in order to lend to His creatures the dignity of causality." Our prayers matter.

"Forgive us our debts, as we also have forgiven our debtors"

More will be said about forgiveness on the next page. For now we can simply note that Jesus made this a matter of importance. Forgiveness opens the door to relationships, both with God and with other people.

"Do not lead us into temptation, but deliver us from evil"

This part of Jesus' prayer has troubled many people. Does God actually tempt us? The word *temptation* in the original language is *peirasmos*. It can mean both "temptation" and "trial." God does not "tempt" people with evil enticement. James 1:13 reads, "Let no one say when he is tempted, 'I am being tempted by God'; for God cannot be tempted by evil, and He Himself does not tempt anyone."

I think Jesus meant that we should pray about the trials that come in our lives. His phrase "do not lead us into temptation" means "do not let us fall into a trial so difficult that we will fail."[5] The issue is testing.

Booker T. Washington wrote in his autobiography, *Up from Slavery*, about the children of his white masters. They were pampered and never taught specific skills. The slaves, though, were taught how to work. After the Civil War, many of the white children who had never learned to work were in trouble because they did not know how to do anything. Most black people knew how to work and could at least make a living. Trials came for both. Some stood up well under the testing while others did not.

The individual petitions in Jesus' Model Prayer end here. The next section is a summary of what needs to be done to keep the door of communication open.

Getting the Attitude Right

Forgiveness is a spiritual nourishment that renews the mind and spirit the way food renews the body. It is a two-way street that carries the traffic of incoming hurt and outgoing pain. Individuals can and should reach out to others and invite them to come close. Forgiveness is thus an open door through which we invite other people to be our neighbors.

Jesus concluded his Model Prayer with these words: "For if you forgive others for their transgressions, your heavenly Father will also forgive you. But if you do not forgive others, then your Father will not forgive your transgressions" (vv. 14–15). These are strong and straightforward words. Make no mistake. Genuine forgiveness is not easy! A library says it "forgives" fines, but that is not really forgiveness. Genuine forgiveness is costly to all involved. It cost God the life of his Son to forgive us. It costs our pride and rebellion to accept it. Forgiveness between people is equally costly because we must open the door to people who have betrayed or hurt us. That is not easy.

The alternative—not to forgive—is even worse. "If you do not forgive others, then your Father will not forgive you." It is that simple and that difficult.

Prayer is too important to leave to chance or to misunderstand. After all, prayer is getting in touch with the Lord of all creation, all time, and all space. What can compare with that? But let's face this fact. Many people have great questions about prayer and think of it as nonsense. Winston Churchill was such a man. In his autobiography he recalled that in his early life he rebelled against faith and prayer. Consider what he said about himself:

> I passed through a violent and aggressive anti-religious phase, which, had it lasted, might easily have made me a nuisance. My poise was restored during the next few years by frequent contact with danger. I found that whatever I might think and argue, I did not hesitate to ask for special protection when about to come under the fire of the enemy; nor to feel sincerely grateful when I got home safe to tea. I even asked for lesser things than not to be killed too soon, and nearly always in these years . . . I got what I wanted. This practice [of prayer] seemed perfectly natural, and just as strong and real as the reasoning process which contradicted it so sharply.[6]

We may never face situations like Churchill did, but we will face our share of crises. Knowing God through prayer will get us through those tough times.

It's Your Turn Now

- Why not use this week as a time to take to heart the meaning of Jesus' prayer?
- You might memorize the prayer.
- You might use the individual petitions for your prayer time. For example, on Monday spend time thinking about the meaning of the phrase "Our Father," and then pray to your heavenly Father. On Tuesday you might think about the phrase "in heaven," and so on.

Questions for Further Reflection and Discussion

1. Why is the prayer Jesus taught called the Model Prayer?

2. What did you learn in this chapter about the various parts of the prayer's petition?

3. Is there anything you think you should not pray for? If so, what?

4. Reflect on the words of Winston Churchill. Can you identify with some of his thoughts?

Read Luke 18:1–14

"I tell you, this man went to his house justified rather than the other; for everyone who exalts himself will be humbled, but he who humbles himself will be exalted."

Luke 18:14

4

Your Attitude Is Important

"Do you believe in prayer?" These words spun in my brain as I answered the phone at 3:00 A.M. The anonymous caller had gotten my name out of the directory and phoned one morning to see if prayer mattered. When the grogginess wore off and I woke up, I questioned the caller about what he meant. He said, "I'm lonesome and I want you to pray that God would send me a wife." I asked him to repeat the request so I could be sure I was not dreaming. He again asked me to pray that God would send him a wife—soon!

We talked on for a few minutes, and I became convinced that he was serious. I began to explain that prayer is not a vending machine in which we automatically get what we want, but my early-morning caller would have none of my explanations. He said just before he hung up, "Look, either prayer works or it doesn't. It's that simple. Now are you going to pray what I asked you for or not?"

I did pray and ask God that this young man could meet a girl, form a deep and lasting relationship, and get married. What I did not do, however, was to request that the Lord send him a wife in the manner that J. C. Penney sends me a package when I order from the catalog.

What attitude should we have when we pray? This is an important question.

Pray with Perseverance

Jesus, the greatest of all teachers, often used simple stories to communicate his message. Stories and parables have a way of getting around people's defenses and entering into the depth of their lives. Luke 18:1–7 forms a parable on prayer. Its purpose is spelled out in verse 1—"that at all times they ought to pray and not to lose heart."

Anyone who has been a Christian for very long and has done much praying knows that discouragement can sometimes set in. We lift our voices to God but seemingly get nothing but silence. Jesus knew that this was the situation, so he taught the disciples to pray in such a manner that they would expect delays. The delays in the answer do not mean that God does not hear, however. Jesus told the disciples that they must never give up as they pray and work. Christians can overcome possible discouragement by continuing to pray, no matter what.

The woman in the parable faced what seemed to be an immovable obstacle—a judge who did not care about justice! He thought of himself as the last word in all matters because he "did not fear God and did not respect man" (v. 2). What happens when a Christian runs up against a brick wall? Do you just stay there? Run? Hide? Back up and hit it again?

Jesus' parable demonstrates that the widow had the kind of attitude needed to succeed in prayer. She would not take "No" for an answer. Her example shows us that perseverance in prayer is characterized by continual, constant praying. Because her need was desperate, the woman kept on asking.

The attitude of seriousness and tenacity is an essential part of the Christian life in general and of prayer in particular. If we approach a problem with the right attitude, we may not get instant results but neither will we get discouraged.

Can we expect anything lasting and worthwhile with little effort and in a short time? A career takes a long time to establish. A relationship takes time and effort to develop. The same is true with prayer. The more we pray, the better able we are to pray. We become more comfortable with this way of expressing ourselves. We also become better able to hear God as he answers us. Even when the answer seems to be silence, we can endure it through persistence.

The judge in the parable decided to act on the widow's behalf, not because he wanted to serve justice, but because he wanted to get rid of this nuisance!

(At least that is what he considered her.) The focal point of the parable is the widow's attitude, not the judge's attitude.

To the judge, power, justice, and authority were commodities to be bought and sold like merchandise. The woman had no cash, no social standing, no power. She just needed and desired to get something done. She hounded the judge day and night until he got tired of her. The old proverb says, "The squeaky wheel gets the grease." In this case, the persistent widow got her desire. The judge reasoned, "Because this widow bothers me, I will give her legal protection, otherwise by continually coming she will wear me out" (v. 5).

If a persistent widow can gain justice from a calloused judge, how much more can a child of God get what he or she needs from God? That is the point of the story. If even a crooked judge can be moved to action by persistence, then certainly a loving heavenly Father will be moved even more by the persistent prayers of his children.

Verses 6 and 7 indicate that God is ready and willing to hear us. "And the Lord said, 'Hear what the unrighteous judge said; now, will not God bring about justice for His elect, who cry to Him day and night, and will He delay long over them?'"

Let me give a personal illustration of this principle of persistent prayer. In 1989 we bought a nice home with four bedrooms and two acres of land. It was just right for our needs. When we were looking for a house, we looked at many but could not find anything we really wanted. When we found this one, my wife and I both said "Yes" immediately. When we went to the mortgage company for a loan, we were assured that there would be no problem and we could close within four weeks. Everything went wrong after that! The loan was supposed to be assumable, but the assumption on the loan was not what the owner had said it was, so we turned it down. That meant we had to start from scratch with a new loan. That took another two months because of the incompetency of the mortgage company.

All the while friends kept asking us, "Are you sure you want that house? Maybe the Lord is trying to tell you something." Their assumption seems to have been that since we had some problems with the loan, perhaps the Lord did not want us to have this house. We kept praying and feeling that he did want us to have this home. So we toughed it out and kept pressing the mortgage company to finish the work. Finally, over three months after we first agreed to buy the house, we moved in.

Just because events do not flow smoothly, do not assume that God is not present in those events. The life of faith is a rocky and rough trail, not a six-lane superhighway. Jesus taught us to pray through difficulties and tough spots.

The seventeenth-century British writer, Samuel Johnson, once wrote:

All the performances of human art, at which we look with praise or wonder, are instances of the resistless force of perseverance: it is by this that the quarry becomes the pyramid, and the distant countries are united with canals. If a man was to compare the effect of a single stroke of the pick-ax, or of one impression of the spade with the general design and last result, he would be overwhelmed by the sense of their disproportion; yet those petty operations incessantly continued, in time surmount the greatest difficulties, and mountains are leveled, and oceans bounded, by the slender force of human beings.[1]

Prayer offered in faith and perseverance is among those strokes that level the mountain.

Pray with Faith

In a "Hagar the Horrible" cartoon, a man in a tuxedo and top hat is shown pulling a wagon loaded with all sorts of trunks. The trunks are labeled with these captions: "Philosophies," "Ideas Big and Small," "Belief Systems," "Notions," "Theories," "Musings," and "Ologies." Hagar's son asks the man with the wagon, "What have you got that's good?"[2] That is an important question. The answer to such a question for us will be "faith."

Jesus said: "I tell you that He will bring about justice for them quickly. However, when the Son of Man comes, will He find faith on the earth?" (Luke 18:8). If perseverance is important in prayer, then faith is even more important.

The widow in the parable kept approaching the judge because she believed that, sooner or later, he would give her what she needed. She had faith that something would happen. In telling the parable, Jesus implied that this same fact remains for people who pray. To pray with persistence and faith is to assure God's notice. This fact is not a "money-back guarantee" that everything will happen just as we want. I could not assure the young man who called me at 3:00 A.M. that the Lord would send him a wife by express mail. What I could do was to tell him that God cared about his dilemma and would work with him.

In November 1960, a six-year-old girl named Ruby Bridges became the first black student in the formerly all-white William T. Frantz school in New Orleans. White parents lined up each day to shout slurs and curses at her as she went to school accompanied by federal marshals. To everyone's amazement, little Ruby did not curse back. She prayed for the adults who lined the street leading to her school. Ruby had been told by her pastor that she should pray for people who persecute her, and she took him at his word. Ruby's mother told a psychologist, "We're not asking her to pray for them because we want to hurt her or anything, but we think that we all have to pray for people like that, and we think Ruby should, too. Don't you think they need praying for?"

Think of it. A six-year-old child taught a city how to pray in faith. The psychiatrist who interviewed Ruby finally concluded that he was mystified by her faith. He wrote, "The great paradox that Christ reminded us about is that sometimes those who are lonely and hurt and vulnerable—*meek*, to use the word—are touched by grace and can show the most extraordinary kind of dignity, and in that sense, inherit not only the next world, but even at times moments of this one. We who have so much knowledge and money and power look on confused, trying to mobilize the intellect, to figure things out. It is not so figurable, is it?"[3]

No, it really is not figurable. The widow in the Bible and the kid in New Orleans trying to go to school displayed an attitude about life that should affect our prayers.

Pray with Humility

The parable of the Pharisee and the tax collector is one of the most familiar in the New Testament. Its very familiarity can cause us trouble, however. Note carefully to whom it was first preached. In verse 9 we learn that Jesus told the parable "to some people who trusted in themselves that they were righteous, and viewed others with contempt."

The tax collectors in Jesus' day were considered traitors to the nation because they helped the nation's enemies. The Pharisees, by contrast, were looked upon as men at the zenith of proper conduct and right attitude. They despised certain people, however, the chief among them being the tax collectors.

Careful now. Part of the Pharisaic attitude in everyone is to look down on others. A person can be a snob about snobs by looking down on people who look down on others! Jesus' point in telling the story was to teach all believers that prayer is reaching out to God. Being in touch with the Creator of the universe is no trifling matter. John Bunyan said centuries ago, "Real prayer is a serious concern, for we are speaking to the Sovereign Lord of all the universe, who is willing to move heaven and earth in answer to sincere and reasonable prayer."

Prayer that centers on our self-righteousness says, "Just look how great I am." This is the attitude Jesus condemned. Why? Because our ego is not the point. I am not the center of the universe—God is. Any attitude that forgets that central fact is misguided.

The tax collector was justified before God because of his attitude. Praying with humility is demonstrated by confessing one's sins and pleading for God's forgiveness. That is what the tax collector did, and that is what Jesus commended.

Part of learning to pray is to humbly discover what Fisher Humphreys calls the three categories of prayer.[4] First, God gives us some things, whether we ask for them or not. He sends the sunshine and rain and oxygen to nourish our planet and us. We do not have to pray for those things. They are part of God's providence.

Second, we ask God for some things he will not grant. He is wiser than we are. Some requests do not fit into his long-range plans for humanity, and others might be harmful to us. Some things we do not get even if we ask.

Third, some things come our way only if we pray. This is the middle ground between the first and second category. For his own purposes, God chooses to grant some things in life only if we ask for those things in prayer.

So what do we ask for? Our ignorance and immaturity often confuse us. We may not know what to ask for. Humphreys suggests that we are driven back to ask for what we think is in keeping with God's will for humankind.

We ask, quite simply, for those things which we believe to be in keeping with God's purposes and thus to be best for ourselves and for those for whom we care: for food and peace for the world, for sensitivity to the needs of those around us, for a good education for our children, for strong and lasting friendships, for a vision of how we may serve God more productively, for healthy families, for guidance for those who must make decisions, for courage for the fearful, hope for the discouraged, wisdom for the confused, and health for the sick.[5]

We ask for what we believe is right. But we humbly admit that sometimes we do not know what is right. Even that can be a matter of prayer.

It's Your Turn Now

As we wrap up this chapter, think about your life right now. Give some thought to some of the challenges you face and face them with prayer. Consider the following personal questions and comments:

- What are the two toughest problems you face right now?
- How can you begin to approach these problems with a healthy attitude?
- Can you, like the widow in the parable, persist in praying about these matters until things change? (Remember, the problems may not change, but your response to them might.)
- Do you have any attitudes that need adjusting?
- You might want to start a prayer diary in which you chart your attitudes, your changes, and the ways God is working in your life.

Questions for Further Reflection and Discussion

1. Have you ever felt like the young man who called at 3:00 A.M. and wanted an answer to prayer right now?

2. What does perseverance in prayer really mean?

3. What does the parable about the unyielding widow and the unjust judge reveal about the character of God?

4. Reflect on the experience of the author's home purchase. Do problems like that have any significance, as if God were trying to tell us something?

5. What does Ruby Bridges have to teach us about our attitudes and prayer?

> ## Read Matthew 5:43–48; 9:35–38; Luke 22:31–32; 23:33–34
>
> "For if you love those who love you, what reward do you have? Do not even the tax collectors do the same? If you greet only your brothers, what more are you doing than others? Do not even the Gentiles do the same? Therefore you are to be perfect, as your heavenly Father is perfect."
>
> Matthew 5:46–48

5

Others Need Your Prayers

"I'LL BE PRAYING FOR YOU." I often hear this statement in my church, and I regularly make it myself.
Somehow, just telling people you are calling their
name before God helps them. The late humorist
Lewis Grizzard learned that fact late in his life when
he underwent serious heart surgery. Grizzard developed complications that almost killed him. He wrote
the following concerning those who cared for him
while he was in the hospital: "To a man and woman,
those doctors and nurses said to me after the critical
time had passed, 'We exhausted all medical possibilities. We did everything we knew to do for you, and it
probably wouldn't have been enough. What saved you
was prayer.'"[1]

Grizzard had another serious problem with
his heart that finally took his life, but he went to
his grave a changed man. After the first heart surgery,

he wrote about all the people who prayed for him. "What I did to deserve any of that I don't know, but I do know I had spent a lot of time in my life doubting. At one time or the other, I doubted it all: spirituality, love, the basic good of humankind. But this flirtation with the end of me has removed a lot of that doubt. If the medical experts say prayer brought me back from certain death, who am I to doubt them?" Grizzard was on to something. He discovered for himself the truth that praying for others *does* make a difference. Life matters. God matters. Love matters.

Blaise Pascal, the seventeenth-century philosopher, once wrote, "When I consider the short duration of my life, swallowed up in the eternity before and after, the little space which I fill and even can see, engulfed in the infinite immensity of spaces of which I am ignorant and which know me not, I am frightened and astonished at being here rather than there; for there is no reason why here rather than there, why now rather than then. Who has put me here? By whose order and direction have this place and time been allotted to me?"[2] Pascal was astonished that he had been given the gift of life at all. I am, too. What further astonishes me is that I have the ability to change my life and the lives of others by prayer. So do you.

Henry David Thoreau wrote, "However mean your life is, meet it and live it; do not shun it and call it hard names. It is not so bad, as you are. It looks poorest when you are richest. The fault-finder will find faults even in paradise. Love your life, poor as it is. Humility, like darkness, reveals the heavenly lights. Superfluous wealth can only buy superfluities. Money is not required to buy any necessary of the soul."[3] Thoreau was on to something. Modest living helps us keep our eyes off ourselves and helps to keep the focus on God. Being focused on something outside ourselves helps us see others as needy children or potential children, of God. We can pray for them and lift them up.

Now that we have established the centrality of prayer in the Christian life and have discussed some other aspects of prayer, we will examine three different groups of people we should include in our prayers. Two groups are expected—Christian workers and our friends. The third group is unexpected—our enemies.

Pray for Christian Workers

One reason why crowds flocked to Jesus, at least early in his ministry, is that the people could sense his care for them. Jesus had compassion on the people because they seemed so helpless and directionless. He cared about what happened to them. Contrast this with the attitude of the Pharisees. The Pharisees were concerned that Jesus was doing things that seemed contrary to Jewish tradition. They were more concerned with their interpretation of the Law than they were with the well-being of the people. The Pharisees downgraded Jesus because he helped the man who was dumb. His action showed his care, whereas their action showed their lack of concern.

The people were like "sheep without a shepherd." Jesus said to his disciples that the people were like a great harvest ready for the scythe blade. All that was needed was a group of committed people to lay the blade to the harvest and gather it in.

Ask God to Send Workers

Jesus instructed his followers to "beseech the Lord of the harvest to send out workers into His harvest." The word translated "beseech" here is translated as "pray" in the Revised Standard Version and as "ask" in the New International Version of the Bible. The meaning is to ask earnestly. To beseech is to want something greatly and to keep asking until you receive it.

Jesus told his disciples to ask the Lord of the harvest—God himself—to send out workers into the ripe fields. God is willing to do his part. Let us do ours, also. We can pray for Christian workers who labor in various fields for the cause of Christ.

The needs of our world are enormous. In fact, the dilemma of people everywhere seems overwhelming at times. This fact only underscores the Christian's need to pray that God would send people to do some harvesting in his fields. We can do that by praying for Christian workers as they take the message of salvation to as many as possible.

Specific Ways to Pray

Here are some specific ways you can pray for Christian workers. First, begin with those closest to you. List the names of your pastor and other leaders in your own church, and pray for them regularly. Next, think of some of the Christian leaders in your area and state who need your prayers.

Do you know any of the leaders of your denomination? Pray for them. Pray next for missionaries, both at home and in foreign places. Now pray for yourself, that you may be one of the Christian workers Christ will use.

Remember that praying is work. It is real, effort-filled toil. You struggle to pray and to keep praying even when you do not see instant results. But Charles Rabon was correct when he wrote, "God has no microwave saints. They aren't made that easily or quickly."[4] Our prayers affect others, but they change us, too.

Pray for Your Friends

How would you like for Jesus himself to pray for you? I can hardly imagine a more impressive spiritual gesture. In Luke's Gospel, Jesus told Simon Peter that he had prayed for him.

The setting was a dispute among Jesus' disciples about who was the greatest. They had not yet learned that in God's eyes, greatness is not a matter of personal pride. Greatness is measured in service to others. Thus, he said, "The one who is the greatest among you must become like the youngest, and the leader like the servant." Jesus said to Peter, "Simon, Simon, behold, Satan has demanded permission to sift you like wheat; but I have prayed for you, that your faith may not fail; and you, when once you have turned again, strengthen your brothers" (Luke 22:31–32).

This prayer was for Jesus' friend and disciple, Simon Peter. We may follow Jesus' example when we pray for our friends' success in overcoming temptation. As a pastor, I personally know when other people are praying for me. I also pray for others who are facing various trials and temptations. Our mutual prayers benefit each other.

Jesus' prayer for Simon helped not only him but others as well. Had Peter failed and turned his back on Christ, many people would not have known of God's love through Peter's later witness. We may never know what wider benefits accrue when we pray for our friends and acquaintances.

Pray for Your Enemies: What Jesus Taught

Anyone, whether Christian or not, can understand the concept of wanting the best for his friends. Many non-Christian people genuinely love their friends and families. These people would have no trouble with Jesus' teaching about praying for friends. What would make them gasp in amazement is the remainder of his teaching. Jesus did not stop at teaching us to pray for our friends. We are also to pray for our enemies!

Jesus' Sermon on the Mount in Matthew 5–7 lays out a blueprint for the kingdom of God. Part of that design calls for his followers to extend their concern beyond their own families and friends. They should reach out even to people they do not like.

Jesus said, "Love your enemies, and pray for those who persecute you." Love your enemies! What a command that is. We might feel more like cursing them or ignoring them. Praying for them is probably the last thing on our minds. But the attitude of the Christian is no longer his own. As Paul put it in Philippians 2:5, "Have this attitude in yourselves which was also in Christ Jesus."

Praying for enemies distinguishes the Christian from everyone else. It is appropriate behavior for followers of Jesus. One person who took this call seriously was a man named Magnus Sacatus Patricius, better known to most as Saint Patrick. He took the gospel to Ireland in the fifth century. Patrick's father was a deacon in the church in Britain, and his influence affected his son. When Patrick was sixteen, the villa he lived in was attacked by pirates from Ireland. The boy and many others were enslaved and carried back to Ireland.

He was sold as a slave to a tribal chieftain who put him to work herding pigs. Patrick remembered his father's teaching about Christ and was converted in this foreign land. He came to be known as "Holy Boy" because of his devotion to God. After six years of slavery, Patrick escaped and made his way home.

After being at home for a while, Patrick surprised his family by telling them that he was going to return to Ireland as Christ's messenger. He wrote in his book, *Confessions*, "I did not go back to Ireland of my own accord. It is not in my own nature to show mercy

toward the very ones who once enslaved me."
Concerning his work as a missionary he wrote, "It was
the furthest thing from me, but God made me fit,
causing me to care about and labor for the salvation
of others."

By the end of his thirty-year ministry in Ireland,
Patrick had seen 100,000 converts and the establish-
ment of many churches. He was someone who took
seriously Christ's words, "Pray for those who persecute
you."

Think about some of the impersonal forces you
consider as enemies, such as poverty, disease, and so
on, that you intend to pray about. Now put some faces
on your enemies and jot down the names of people
you consider enemies (or at least non-friends). Make
it a point to pray for them this week.

Pray for Your Enemies: What Jesus Did

I sometimes hear people say things like, "Jesus
was a good teacher, but nothing more." They seem to
assume that Jesus' teaching and actions did not mesh
perfectly. He taught people to pray for their enemies.
Saying this while comfortable and safe, as on the
mountainside surrounded by disciples, is one thing.
Practicing it under horrible conditions is quite another.

On the final day of his earthly life, Jesus was crucified on a cross. This was a tortuous death. If he were
ever to go back on his teaching, surely it would have
been at that time. But look at what happened. Luke
23:34 records, "But Jesus was saying, 'Father, forgive

them; for they do not know what they are doing.'" He not only taught that one should pray for his enemies; he set the example himself.

I heard of a letter that was found in a baking powder can wired to the handle of an old pump. The pump offered the only drinking water on a long and seldom-used trail across the Amargosa Desert. The letter read:

> This pump is all right as of June 1932. I put a new sucker washer into it and it ought to last five years. But the washer dries out and the pump has got to be primed. Under the white rock I buried a bottle of water, out of the sun and cork end up. There's enough water to prime the pump, but not if you drink some first. Pour about one fourth and let her soak the leather. Then pour in the rest medium fast and pump like crazy. You'll git water. The well has never run dry. Have faith. When you git watered up, fill the bottle and put it back like you found it for the next feller. [signed] Desert Pete.[5]

Praying for an enemy is a lot like that pump. It is an act of faith that "primes the pump" in relationships. It also gives something to the coming generation because it helps break the cycle of hate and fear. It's tough! But it's necessary.

It's Your Turn Now

The title of this chapter, "Others Need Your Prayers," is a statement of fact. We have considered several ways you can put into effect the central truth of this fact. Here are several other suggestions that may also help you better pray for others.

- Thank God for the times when others have prayed for you.
- Make a prayer list of the names of people and situations you know could use your prayers. Keep this list up to date. That is, add and delete names and situations as needed.
- Read other books on prayer.
- Attend prayer meetings with other people.
- Most importantly, pray that God would use you as a Christian worker. Be careful what you pray for, though. You might get it.

Questions for Further Reflection and Discussion

1. What does it mean to ask God to send workers?

2. Imagine that Jesus is praying for you. What difference do you think that would make?

3. Is praying for your enemies realistic today? Was it ever realistic?

4. Can you think of one or two people you might classify as an enemy? Pray for (not against) them once a day for a week and see what happens.

Read Jeremiah 11:18–12:6; 20:7–18

"If you have run with footmen and they have tired you out, then how can you compete with horses? If you fall down in a land of peace, how will you do in the thicket of the Jordan?"

Jeremiah 12:5

6

Honesty in Prayer

"IF GOD KNEW how I really felt, I'm not sure what he would do." Thus began a conversation with a friend on the nature of God and the friend's doubts. We were not long into the conversation before I discovered that this friend felt like he was the only person having difficulty with faith. To his relief I showed him that others, even in the Bible, have had trouble with their religious commitments. Jeremiah was one such person. For him, faith was not an escape from reality. It was just the opposite—a movement toward the source of all truth and reality. That source is God.

In this chapter we will look at the matter of honesty toward God in prayer. We will examine what the prophet Jeremiah had to say about his encounters with God and his fellow countrymen. From that we will discover many truths about prayer, but one will especially stand out—prayer is radical honesty.

My friend's comment is important. First, he thought that God did not know how he felt—"If God knew. . . ." Second, he thought that even if God did know, the Lord would be angry and/or disappointed. Third, he felt that the road to faith and piety lay in hiding feelings and doubts rather than exposing them to the fresh air of Scripture, shared wisdom, and honest prayer. In short, my friend, and probably countless others, wondered about this fundamental question of faith: "Can I be completely honest with God and tell him my doubts and complaints as well as my faith and strength?"

An excellent way to get at that question is by examining the life and teaching of the prophet Jeremiah, a man of deep feeling. He grieved over the status of his country and its plunge into disaster. He was no "armchair quarterback" but was in the game at all times. This strong and sensitive man was honest with himself about his feelings. He made no attempt to hide or bury them. This openness led him also to be honest with God. We see Jeremiah struggling with doubts compounded with feelings that God was unfair.

Piety or Blasphemy?

To some contemporary Christians fed on the cotton candy fluff of some modern teaching, Jeremiah's words sound like blasphemy. His comment is not a "name it and claim it" boost. It has no "victory" sound to it. Did the prophet stand with white marks on his sandals as he inched up to the chalk mark separating honesty from blasphemy? Part of the answer can be found by examining the opening of chapter 12.

Jeremiah began his prayer, not with rage or impertinence, but with a reverent salutation: "Righteous are You, O LORD. . . ." (Jer. 12:1). Only after such a greeting could he then lay out his feelings before God. The mood reminds us of Jesus in the Garden of Gethsemane on the night of his arrest. He prayed, "Father, if You are willing, remove this cup from Me; yet not My will, but Yours be done" (Luke 22:42).

Jeremiah did not accuse God of injustice. He did not bring a case *against* God, but rather *before* Him. The prophet pled his case with God. What was the problem? He was troubled about the matter of justice, or, in this case, what seemed like injustice: "Why has the way of the wicked prospered?" (v. 1). Jeremiah looked around him and saw his nation falling apart. Trouble seemed to be brewing on every side. The godly, although seeming to be in small numbers, were not faring well. The ungodly, in vast numbers, seemed to prosper. Jeremiah could not understand it. He wondered if God was diligent about the matters of earth. This question of injustice is expressed in other places in the Bible, most notably in the Psalms.

Psalm 73:1–14 is a good example. The first five verses read, "Surely God is good to Israel, to those who are pure in heart! But as for me, my feet came close to stumbling, my steps had almost slipped. For I was envious of the arrogant as I saw the prosperity of the wicked. For there are no pains in their death, and their body is fat. They are not in trouble as other men, nor are they plagued like mankind." This situation seemed to be a reversal of the rules. The righteous were supposed to prosper and the wicked were supposed to vanish, weren't they?

It did not work out that way for Jeremiah, and it often does not today. Sometimes the roles seem reversed, almost to the point of appearing as if the wicked are supposed to prosper! I have a friend who worked on an oil drilling rig in Louisiana. He felt a call to become a minister and accepted it. On his last day on the rig before going back to school, a piece of steel fell out of the derrick and struck my friend on the side of the head. He is damaged for life and has no chance to fulfill his call. Why do the righteous suffer?

On the other hand, I heard of two brothers who owned a men's store in New York. If someone came in to look at suits, one brother would wait on him. If the customer asked, "How much is this suit?" the man waiting on him would say, "I don't know. Let me find out." Then he would yell across the store, "Hey Mort, how much is this gray pinstripe?" His brother would yell back, "$199.95." Then the first brother working with the customer would pretend to be hard of hearing and say to the customer, "Mort says it's $139.95." The customer, who just heard the price quoted at $199.95, thought he was getting a steal and would buy the suit immediately. Why do those who do not play straight prosper? Only God knows.

Jeremiah's preaching was not well received by his countrymen. The people of false piety in his hometown of Anathoth (12:2) and even his own family (12:6) did not want the prophet's message. They had even plotted against his life (11:19). All of this came after he tried to serve God faithfully but seemed to get nowhere. Thus, his complaint in 12:1 came pouring out.

People of genuine faith may address their doubts and questions to God in prayer. This is what Jeremiah did, and what we today may do. It is not blasphemy to raise genuine questions and doubts to God. It is instead a sign of deep trust.

God's Answer

When Jeremiah spoke openly to God, the Lord returned the favor. He spoke freely to the prophet. The answer God provided in Jeremiah 12:5 is something for which Jeremiah was not searching. Perhaps he expected the Lord to say something like this: "Yes, Jeremiah, you are right. I've been negligent, but I promise to do better. From now on, you can rest assured that I will be watching out for you a little better." After all, had not Jeremiah committed his life and work to God? (See 11:20.)

God's answer to Jeremiah is more a challenge than an easy answer. He challenged the prophet to grow, to get stronger, to prepare himself for the future battles, which would be much tougher than the ones already fought. James Leo Green has paraphrased God's answer in verse 5 this way: "If a few footrunners have worn you out in your race for me, what will you do when you come up against thoroughbred horses? And if you fall flat on your face on level ground in a pleasant meadowland as you move for me, what will you do in the tangled, lion-infested jungles of the Jordan? The days are coming which will make these days look like easy days. There are higher hurdles ahead. You are up against boys now. There are men farther down the road, and farther still, giants. Cheer up, Jeremiah, the worst is yet to come!"[1] What comfort!

One who reads the Bible seriously will learn quickly that God seldom gives simple, trite answers to our questions. Instead, he challenges us to grow and develop spiritually. He wanted Jeremiah to get stronger in his smaller trials so that when the larger ones came, he would be ready. Genuine prayer, as I have indicated before, is no trivial pursuit.

Think back over the last two years of your life. Have you encountered anything you might consider as "light" trials, which might prepare you for things to come? Perhaps you have already felt overwhelmed and hope nothing worse comes along. Why not make this concern a matter of prayer? Speak openly to God about it. But remember, you may get an unexpected answer.

Accusing God!

You have to hand it to Jeremiah. Whatever else he might have been, he was not a coward. After his initial complaint in 12:1, he moved on in his relationship to

God. As that relationship grew and developed, so did the prophet's boldness. In 20:7 we see Jeremiah accusing God of deceit: "O LORD, You have deceived me and I was deceived; You have overcome me and prevailed. I have become a laughingstock all day long."

This accusation, which runs from verse 7 through verse 18, has been called "one of the most powerful and impressive passages in the whole of the prophetic literature, a passage which takes us, as no other, not only into the depths of the prophet's soul, but into the secrets of the prophetic consciousness."[2]

Although Jeremiah felt deceived, he at least felt that God was doing this for some purpose. Even so, this passage illustrates the suffering involved in living one's life in faithfulness to God. The word *deceived* in verse 7 is used in Exodus 22:16 for the rape of a virgin and in Judges 16:5 of Delilah's seduction of Samson. Jeremiah felt that God had seduced, enticed, and tricked him into surrendering his life. That caused Jeremiah great anguish later on. We can imagine why. If God is not trustworthy, who is?

Jeremiah felt a deep personal hurt. Not only did he feel abandoned by friends and family, but he also felt tricked by God. When a person feels this low, there is nowhere else to go but up. But the climb back up was not accomplished in an instant, or even in a day. It took Jeremiah a lifetime to come to terms with his circumstances. He poured out his anger and sense of outrage to God all the while.

Do you see how Jeremiah's circumstances relate

to prayer? Earlier I called prayer "radical honesty." Jeremiah was certainly honest with God, honest enough to wonder if God was having a bellylaugh at his expense. Was the whole business a kind of celestial joke? What was going on? Jeremiah, like many before and after him, began to realize that prayer is no child's game. C. S. Lewis once said, "Prayer is either a sheer illusion or a personal contact between embryonic, incomplete persons (ourselves) and the utterly con-crete Person."[3]

Rejection and Betrayal

To feel tricked by God is bad enough, but to feel cut off from friends and family compounds the wound. Jeremiah had known that some members of his family had rejected him (12:6) and some had even plotted to kill him (11:19). He stood up under this pressure for a while, but it began to get to him. In 20:8 and 10 he expressed his great hurt to God. Jeremiah said in verse 8 that he had faithfully done his duty as he under-stood it. In the previous verse he noted that he had become a laughingstock for the people. No one likes to be ridiculed! It is a painful thing to be laughed at, but to be scorned when you think you are doing God's will is even harder to take! Yet this was Jeremiah's trouble.

He said that each time he spoke, he proclaimed violence and destruction. But what did his faithfulness to his Lord get him? Laughter and ridicule. The peo-ple did not want a word of judgment and woe. They wanted someone to tell them they would be victorious. Jeremiah's preaching had little effect other than to antagonize the people.

In verse 10 he related to the Lord that the people had made a joke of his preaching. Can't you just hear them as they would say something like this? "Hey look, there's old 'Terror-on-every-side.' Come on. Let's have some fun. Hey, 'Terror,' what news do you have for us today? Are we going to fall today?" This would be followed by peals of laughter from the people. Ridiculing is always easier than working. Sneering is less costly than being faithful. The majority of the people thought of Jeremiah as little more than an anachronism, a stage-joke to be scorned. He said, "All my trusted friends, watching for my fall, say: 'Perhaps he will be deceived, so that we may prevail against him and take our revenge on him'" (v. 10c). Thus Jeremiah knew scorn, the abandonment of friends and family, and plots against him.

How did Jeremiah stand up under such pressure? The answer to this question is found in the last part of verse 12: "For to You I have set forth my cause." Why did he remain steadfast in the midst of his suffering?

- He believed that God was with him (v. 11).
- He felt that because he was on God's side, his enemies would not prevail.
- He thought that the Lord knew his heart and mind and the hearts and minds of his detractors.

His position was neither easy nor enviable, but he did not give up even though he was tempted to quit.

Tempted to Quit

A friend of mine left the professional ministry several years ago. Many relationships in his life soured. Neither work nor home was a source of comfort or joy. He resigned his position, divorced his wife, and moved to another state and began working for a secular organization. This man's name could be Legion, for he is many. Each year hundreds of ministers resign their positions and enter secular work. They get burned out and used up. While the term *burnout* seems to be new, the condition it describes is as old as Jeremiah.

In verse 9 the prophet expressed his desire to stop preaching. What good had it done? All he could see was the pain it caused him. We should remember that this verse is set in the larger context of a prayer that Jeremiah offers to God, which begins at verse 7 and ends with verse 18. This prayer is well in keeping with his honesty and openness to his Lord.

He said, "But if I say, 'I will not remember Him or speak anymore in His name,' then in my heart it becomes like a burning fire shut up in my bones; and I am weary of holding it in, and I cannot endure it." Jeremiah was telling the one who had called and commissioned him that he had had enough. The experience was too painful. The prophet found, however, that he could not turn off the inner conviction of his heart the way we today turn off a light switch. Whenever he tried to stop thinking about God or speaking in his name, Jeremiah found that he could not control his mind. He could not forget.

Like a fire burning inside him, a fire that could not be contained, the word of God kept demanding expression. Jeremiah found that he was not in control any longer. This does not mean that he was a mere robot or puppet controlled by God. Instead, the message from his Lord had become so much a part of Jeremiah that he could not cut it off without injuring himself. His sense of calling was real, and his relationship with God was so deep and personal that it was too intertwined in his life to forget it.

As I stated before, I am married and have twin teenage sons. Most of the time I am very happy in my homelife, but sometimes I get angry or disappointed. Suppose I said one day, "Well, if that's the way you're going to treat me, I'll just leave." I pack my suitcase and leave. What would happen the next day? This has never happened in my home, but I am sure I would go right back. Why? My relationships with my wife and children are too much a vital part of my life simply to forget or turn off.

This simple illustration is, I think, something that will offer a clue to verse 9. Jeremiah wanted to do what was right. He had a deep and abiding faith in God, and he spoke what he believed to be God's message to his fellow countrymen. All he got for his trouble was ridicule. He thought about abandoning his prophetic vocation, but found he had been with it too long. It had become a living part of him and not just something he did out of expectation or coercion.

God's word lived in him, and it bubbled to the surface and demanded expression. However we think about this, the important thing to realize is that Jeremiah was saying two important things at the same time. First, he was stating his fatigue and stress; from them came his comment about wanting to stop speaking in God's name. Second, he was indicating that his relationship with God was too deep to lay aside. He felt too strongly about his prophetic vocation simply to abandon it. His words sound like Paul in 1 Corinthians 9:16 when he said, "Woe is me if I do not preach the gospel." This is both divine compulsion and personal expression.

Christians today face this same dilemma as Jeremiah. We sometimes feel tired and at the end of our ropes. We get weary of trying to be lighthouses in a dark world, of turning the other cheek while others take advantage of us, of always giving while others seem only to get. When we reach this state, remembering Jeremiah will help us. As God rekindled his sense of call, so the Lord can renew our sense of call and commission.

Does this lesson apply to you personally? To someone you know well? Consider ways you might open yourself to God's renewing of your relationship to him. Keeping a relationship open to God in prayer is not always easy. As you grow in your faith, you will experience times that seem silent. But don't give up. Like Jeremiah, your faith can be renewed.

Renewed Faith

After all the complaining, after all the expression of deceit, after all the feelings of dread, Jeremiah came finally to realize that his situation was not hopeless. He felt himself answerable to God, and at the same time, he felt that God was answerable to him. This mutual accountability was not arrogance on Jeremiah's part. It was an expression of his faith that God would not leave him alone and defenseless. God would answer him and come to him. Verse 11 is the prophet's confession of faith. God was with him, and his enemies would not prevail against him.

Jeremiah called the Lord a "dread champion." The word *champion* means "warrior." By calling the Lord a "dread champion," Jeremiah expressed his belief that, despite all the setbacks and the ups and downs of his faith, he still believed that God would be his champion or warrior. God would assure the victory of his faith.

This description of God as a warrior sounds strange to the ears of contemporary Christians. We are nursed on the milk of peace and harmony. We are nurtured on the solid food of Jesus' words about turning the other cheek. What could Jeremiah's description of God in such a military fashion mean? The words of Elizabeth Achtemeier might be helpful here. This theologian wrote:

> . . . it is a description of God's person essential to the biblical witness. Jeremiah's God is at war against Judah's sin, just as surely as he is also at war against ours. Jeremiah has heard the sounds and seen the sights of that coming war . . . and they are dreadful in their portent. Jeremiah knows, according to the words of this confession, that God's judgment on Judah will come and that therefore his preaching of doom will be vindicated, while those who scorn his message will be eternally dishonored, as they are at this day. God is not Lord unless he wars against human defiance of him, and he is not good except he be also an enemy of our evil. So over against all our attempts to have it our own way, over against every desire of ours to compromise his will, stands this dread Warrior God of this prophet of Judah.[4]

God was thus the "dread champion" for Jeremiah in that he was (and still is) at war with sin. The prophet's confidence in God's saving presence raised him up out of his sense of despair. As we have seen, Jeremiah felt that he had been deceived about what God was doing and what God required of him. When he saw the wicked prosper, he wondered if God had not made some mistake! Finally, however, Jeremiah thought seriously about the nature of God. He realized that, contrary to appearances, God was still in charge. The history of Judah was unfolding to indicate that God was indeed at war with rebellion and sin. Jeremiah tried to get his people to see that they were digging their own graves.

In all of this, Jeremiah was open in his relationship with God. He was so open, in fact, that his honesty is transparent. The ancient prophet has much to teach contemporary Christians in this regard. For Jeremiah, the opposite of reverence is not honesty, but apathy. We need not be overly concerned about "offending" God with our honesty. I am not suggesting that we treat God disrespectfully! My point is that deep belief creates strong convictions and feelings. These convictions and feelings are sometimes contradicted and opposed by certain events in our world. We sometimes hear well-meaning people say, "Just pray and everything will be all right." But not everything is all right. Loved ones die. We have financial struggles and setbacks. Personal relationships get fouled up.

The trouble with this simplistic thinking is that it is not biblical. Jeremiah knew that no amount of false piety would ever bring him to a deeper understanding of God's purposes in this world. Read the first eight chapters of Job and Paul's letter to the Philippians. You will discover two men wrestling with things that have gone wrong. But you will also discover two men who were honest with God and who would not give up. Such was the case with Jeremiah. Like Jacob wrestling with the angel at Jabbok (Gen. 32:24–32), Jeremiah refused to give up until he was blessed.

It's Your Turn Now

We can learn to pray by thinking of our prayers as speaking to an intimate friend. True friendship rests on honesty. A deep faith relationship does, too. This honesty does not insult God or make him any less God. It draws us closer to him and lets us know that he understands and cares. God cares. He really cares. This is the greatest lesson we can learn from Jeremiah. Furthermore,

- Honesty can be reverent and reverence can be honest.
- God is tough enough to hear any question we have or to shoulder any feeling we bring to him.
- Our pilgrimage of faith and prayer is not a smooth road. It is often a rocky, rut-filled path through the wilderness.
- We grow the most when, like Jeremiah, we find our ideas challenged and we have to keep relearning about God.
- In order to put into practice what you have learned, you might want to begin keeping a prayer journal. This is a notebook in which you record your prayers and answers to your prayers. It would include honest questions

and deep feelings, such as Jeremiah had. You might just find your prayer life revolutionized by using a prayer journal.

Questions for Further Reflection and Discussion

1. Are you shocked and disturbed or comforted at Jeremiah's honesty with God?

2. Have there been times when you felt betrayed by everyone, including God?

3. This chapter began with this sentence: "If God knew how I really felt, I'm not sure what he would do." How do you react to such a statement?

4. God's answer to Jeremiah's complaints do not seem very soft or comforting. What do you think God was trying to teach Jeremiah?

5. Have there been times when you, like Jeremiah, have been tempted to quit serving God or trying to learn more about him?

6. Jeremiah called God a "dread champion." What does that mean?

Read Matthew 26:36–46

He went away again a second time and prayed, saying, "My Father, if this cannot pass away unless I drink it, Your will be done."

Matthew 26:42

7
God Will Strengthen You Through Prayer

"OH, GOOD, you're not busy." That is the tag line on a cartoon that shows a pastor in his study. He is kneeling in prayer as the secretary comes in with a handful of papers. She looks down, sees the pastor praying, and says, "Oh, good, you're not busy."

What do you make of this situation? Is he busy with something momentous and urgent, or is he just fiddling with some trifle until he has something better to do? I can answer that question from my own experience as a minister. Without prayer, I'm as good as dead.

We human beings are weak and needy creatures because we are so complex and full of potential. Our very potential marks us for temptation and weakness. Temptations are downward pulls that touch us at important points in our lives. We are seldom tempted with something unimportant. For instance, sexual temptations are strong and persistent. People are vulnerable to this problem because the Lord himself made us sexual beings and said to Adam and Eve, "Be fruitful and multiply." This was the only divine command that humanity has taken up with gusto! The point here is that sexuality is a major and vital aspect of our lives. We are susceptible to falling just because it is so important.

In all times of testing, temptation, and grief we can seek spiritual strength through prayer. Throughout the previous chapters on prayer we have discovered that prayer is not magic or a gimmick that allows us to get whatever we desire. Prayer is our heart communicating with the heart of God. It is our mind pouring itself out to the mind of God. Prayer is essentially personal in that it takes all that we are and gives it to God. Jesus shows us how to pray when we need God's strength.

Pray to Do God's Will

If you knew you were about to die, what would you do? This was not an academic question for Jesus as he took his disciples to Gethsemane. He knew that something was about to break. He had come to die for mankind and was preparing to see the end of his desire.

Jesus took the eleven disciples to the garden. He stationed eight of them at a key position and took Peter, James, and John to a more central location. The Scripture says Jesus "began to be grieved and distressed. Then He said to them, 'My soul is deeply grieved, to the point of death; remain here and keep watch with Me.'" Here was Jesus himself, the very Son of God, in grief and anguish. How did he deal with his dilemma? He prayed.

Prayer is sometimes a wrestling match of the soul, a wrestling match with God. Jesus told a parable about an unjust judge to teach that people should keep praying and searching and not give up (Luke 18:1–8). This perseverance is often called importunity. Curtis Mitchell has written, "Importunity is an instructor in God's school of Christian development. In short, God does not become more willing to answer because of perseverance, but the petitioner may become more capable of receiving the answer."[1]

I think the late British theologian P. T. Forsyth was on target when he wrote, "Lose the importunity of prayer, reduce it to soliloquy, or even colloquy, with God, lose the real conflict of will and will, lose the habit of wrestling and the hope of prevailing with God, make it mere walking with God in friendly talk; and precious as it is, yet you tend to lose the reality of prayer at last."[2] Life's most important decisions require life's most important resources. One of those is prayer.

Jesus could have done other things. He could have called in the legions of angels to help him. He could have given up on mankind and let everyone be damned. But with the entire arsenal of heaven at his disposal, Jesus chose prayer as the one right weapon with which to fight this battle. It was right because prayer helps to establish and maintain a relationship with God. Prayer helps us do the things of God in God's way. God's way is to love human beings. Jesus prayed so that he could love us enough to do whatever it took, even being crucified on a cross.

If prayer was right for Jesus, then it is equally right for us. Praying for spiritual strength is appropriate in times of grief and distress. When death comes to loved ones, pray. When temptations come, pray. When plans are shattered, pray. Prayer is personal communication between you and God. It can never be out of place.

Matthew tells us that Jesus went a bit further away from his three closest friends and prayed more. The content of that prayer shows the difference between prayer that is self-centered and prayer that is God-centered. Jesus said, "My Father, if it is possible, let this cup pass from Me; yet not as I will, but as You will" (v. 39). The "cup" spoken of here was the total experience of anguish Jesus felt and his death on a cross shortly to take place.

In one sense Jesus did not want to die. Like any man, he wanted to live as long as possible. Thus he prayed, "if it is possible, let this cup pass from Me." In another sense, though, he realized that life was more than protecting himself. Thus he continued, "yet not as I will, but as You will." The word yet made all the difference in the world. He wanted relief and deliverance, but he was willing to accept whatever came because he trusted God. Jesus felt the great anguish of the occasion and, in a way, wanted out of it. Even so, he could say to God, "Yet I do not choose my way, but I choose your way."

Praying to *know* God's will is one thing. Praying to *do* God's will is something else. We will explore this matter further in the next chapter. Here let us simply realize that knowing the will of God is only the first step in the process. Doing his will requires faith and courage. We Christians should pray to find God's strength in times of stress. But we should also commit ourselves to do God's will regardless of the outcome.

I once tried to talk to a man about God. He told me that when he was young his grandmother, with whom he lived, became ill. He prayed that she would get well, but she died. He said, "If God is real and hears prayer, why didn't he answer me?" Anyone can pray, but not everyone is prepared to accept God's answer. That man did not seem to realize that God had said "no" to his prayer. Jesus' prayer in Gethsemane indicates that he knew the difference between calling on God to get our way and calling on him to find his way. We may legitimately call upon the Lord for anything that concerns us. We should seek what God wants for us so we can do his will. This is not always easy, but it is always important.

Pray to Resist Temptation to Sin

"And He came to the disciples and found them sleeping" (v. 40). These words arrest our attention as we consider the momentous decisions being made and the actions being planned that night.[3] Jesus was in one of the toughest spiritual battles of his life. He was planning for victory. The Pharisees had gotten a mob together to arrest Jesus. They were planning for revenge. And the disciples? They were not planning for anything.

Jesus indicated that Peter and the others could not stay awake for even one hour. Before we think too lowly of the disciples, let us remember that all the events of that final week in Jesus' life had been extremely stressful for everyone involved. The disciples were fatigued and needed rest. They were exhausted from sorrow. Jesus knew that fatigue pulls people off guard. We are simply not at our best and as careful as we should be when we are tired.

Jesus said, "Keep watching and praying that you may not enter into temptation; the spirit is willing, but the flesh is weak." Prayer keeps us on our guard against temptations to sin. Temptation itself is not sin. A temptation is a suggestion or an urge. We cannot always control temptations, but Jesus warns us to be on guard against surrendering to temptations. C. H. Spurgeon, a nineteenth-century British Baptist, used to say, "I cannot prevent the birds of temptation from flying over my head, but I can prevent them from building a nest in my hair!"

There are passive sins as well as active sins. Some sins we commit by actually doing something, but others we commit by doing nothing. The sleeping disciples remind us that Christians fall into some sin, not because they do something wrong, but because they do nothing at all. You have probably heard someone pray, "O Lord, please forgive us the sins of commission and omission."

"Get real!" a person once told me when I was speaking about prayer. She continued, "Prayer is OK and it makes you feel good. But in the real world it doesn't make any difference. Does prayer really help when we face tough problems?" Yes, prayer really helps us when temptations and trials come. Prayer is not a magic carpet that zips us away from the trouble. It is an internal communication that helps us realize we are not alone in our struggles. Prayer has many beneficial effects. Let us consider one example of the benefits.

Dr. Herbert Benson, a professor at Harvard Medical School, has identified what he calls the "faith factor" in physical and emotional healing. The "faith factor" is the natural healing process that is made possible by the interaction of two forces. The first is a strong personal belief system that accepts the importance of caring for the body. The second is the practice of prayer and meditation as a part of that belief system.[4] Benson discovered that people with firm religious or philosophical convictions who practice meditative prayer have the most success in healing certain conditions. These conditions include high blood pressure, headaches, backaches, and mental depression.

Dr. Kenneth Cooper, who brought the word *aerobics* into common use, discovered the same thing. Cooper reviewed Benson's work and the research of others and came away with these observations: "As a Christian and a physician, I find such research to be quite encouraging because I do believe that there is a continuum between natural and supernatural healing. It makes sense to me that deep faith, enhanced by a developed life of prayer and meditation, would have a positive influence on the way our God-given bodies function and heal."[5]

Prayer helps to heal the body and the spirit. It helps us know we are not just some fluke of nature or an orphan in the universe. Prayer is real, and so are its results.

Continue Praying for God's Will

Very little in the spiritual life is easy. Make no mistake about that. Life in the Spirit is often difficult (but, of course, life in general is difficult). The Bible tells us something very important about this. Jesus himself prayed three different times in his struggle to do God's will. Consider Luke's version of this night. He wrote, "And being in agony He was praying very fervently; and His sweat became like drops of blood, falling down upon the ground" (22:44). That does not sound like a snap, does it?

What are we to make of this fact? Why would Jesus pray like that? Read the entire story in the New Testament and you will discover that Jesus was a real man. Yes, he was unique—the very Son of God. But he was flesh and blood, too. The early church referred to Jesus as "fully man, fully God." He *struggled* in the

Garden of Gethsemane about his destiny. The battle going on in his mind was not a shame fight. He wrestled with all the normal human emotions and desires that others have, but he also fought to keep focused on the most important fact, namely, what God willed. Prayer helped Jesus to affirm his mission and to continue with it.

In Matthew 26 we read that Jesus prayed a second time. During this time of prayer, he came to the momentous conclusion of his life and ministry: "My Father, if this cannot pass away unless I drink it, Your will be done" (v. 42). The key is the phrase, "Your will be done." He prayed a third time in a similar manner. After fervent prayer Jesus was willing to accept whatever was to come. He certainly knew that a cross awaited him.

If Jesus needed to keep praying about doing God's will, what about us? Was he so special and his work so unique that only he had to pray regularly about doing what his heavenly Father wanted? If Jesus needed regular, fervent prayer, how much more do we!

What do you really want out of life? Are you striving all alone to achieve your goals? Prayer is not just a tool that allows you to get what you want from life. It is communion with the divine will. As you pray about finding and doing God's will, let the Lord lead you in your life's goals and dreams. Keep praying about this matter.

Jesus prayed not only twice but three times about his decision in the Garden of Gethsemane. He prayed about his impending death three times. Some events and decisions in life are too important for quick, shallow thought. They require sustained and repeated prayer. Praying for spiritual strength to do God's will is so important that it needs to be done repeatedly.

Pray to Find Spiritual Strength

If you had been one of Jesus' disciples that night, what would you have done? We might fantasize that we would have stayed awake with Jesus. None of us were there, of course, but we face other trials regularly. Sometimes we are alert and on top, but sometimes we are like old Rip van Winkle, who slept through a revolution.

Jesus faced his most trying hour in Gethsemane. His prayers strengthened him to face that time. Our greatest challenges can be met with similar resources.

Praying for spiritual strength to do God's will should include a commitment to do it, no matter what. Jesus was committed to carry out God's will, regardless of the consequences. If you pray to discover God's will, be prepared to do it. Otherwise, why bother?

It's Your Turn Now

What is the one most challenging issue facing you right now? Based on this study of Jesus' example of prayer, use the following questions to design a prayer strategy to deal with this challenge.

- What is God's will for the challenge you listed? How can you keep on praying until you find his will and his strength to assist you in this dilemma?
- What are some other challenges in life right now?
- Think of some of the struggles and temptations you have faced over the past two weeks. Did prayer help you in any of them?
- If you did not pray during those times, make up your mind now to ask for God's help this week as you face whatever comes your way.

Questions for Further Reflection and Discussion

1. Think of the cartoon mentioned at the beginning of this chapter. Can you identify with it?

2. Why do you think Jesus prayed so earnestly over his decision in the Garden of Gethsemane?

3. In what ways can prayer help you during times of temptation?

4. Reflect on the research of Dr. Herbert Benson and Dr. Kenneth Cooper regarding the relationship of faith, prayer, and health. Are there any changes you might need to make in your life to maximize the benefits of faith and prayer?

Read Ephesians 5:18–21

"And do not get drunk with wine, for that is dissipation, but be filled with the Spirit, speaking to one another in psalms and hymns and spiritual songs, singing and making melody with your heart to the Lord; always giving thanks for all things in the name of our Lord Jesus Christ to God, even the Father; and be subject to one another in the fear of Christ."

Ephesians 5:18–21

8

Prayer and God's Will
For Your Life

WE HAVE BEEN LOOKING at the biblical concept of
prayer throughout this book. We began by looking at
some of the common misunderstandings about prayer.
Then we considered the invitation that comes to each
of us to become people of prayer. Next, we looked at
one way of praying, and then we explored the importance of our attitude toward prayer life. We also
looked at the fact that others need our prayers as
much as we do. Then we examined the life of
Jeremiah to discover the open, almost shocking honesty needed for prayer.

Now we are going to pull together much of what
we examined earlier and ask this simple question:
Where does prayer fit in with God's will for my life? Let
us consider this question by briefly exploring the general nature of God's will.

God's General Will

There is much confusion about the concept of God's will. Some people think of God's will as being a target with a bull's-eye. The key, they think, is to fire at the target and hit the center every time. Any shot outside the bull's-eye is thus a shot outside of God's perfect will. Is that an accurate image of God's will? I do not believe it is.

To begin with, we need to reexamine some of the phrases that are often used in connection with God's will, phrases such as "God showed me," "discern the Lord's mind," "the very center of his will," and so on. Theologian Gary Friesen makes a strong statement about these and other similar phrases. He writes, "Such terminology reflects the conviction that the key to making the 'right' decision is discernment of God's ideal plan. What is so striking, as one searches the pages of the New Testament, is the *glaring absence* of such expressions."[1]

Friesen points out that the New Testament does not approach the will of God with the metaphor of an archer hitting a bull's-eye. Instead, it pictures Christians who use their minds to perceive what God has revealed for all people. Friesen's argument continues: "In the progress of His revelation, God moved from a highly structured system of regulations governing a wide range of specific behaviors to a system where behavior is to be determined by principles and governed by personal relationship. There was a progress from law to Christ; from the bondage of close, restrictive supervision appropriate to immature and willful children to the freedom of responsible adulthood."[2]

The apostle Paul wrote about our movement from the restrictive bondage of childhood to the open freedom of Christ. Read his comments in Galatians 4:1–11. This kind of mature freedom is not possible for everyone, of course.

I wrote this chapter at a church camp in Ridgecrest, North Carolina. Outside my window several young adults were busy sweeping the walks and picking up trash. All of them are mentally handicapped. A supervisor must be with them at all times to offer specific guidance. However, if those employees were mature and capable of handling themselves, having a supervisor stand over them and tell them everything to do would be irritating and degrading, because mature people are capable of thinking for themselves and making their own decisions from many options.

This illustration is not a perfect analogy, of course, but I think that God is nurturing his children toward maturity. In that maturity, coupled with the wisdom he gives us, we are responsible for making wise decisions from all the possibilities that come our way.

I think Friesen is on to something here. He articulates what others have also discovered. God intends his children to grow up and use their wisdom to discern what he wants them to do. Many people approach the idea of God's will as if they think that all people remain infants who need to be taken by the hand and walked all the way through life. But the Scriptures call us to grow up in our faith and to use our God-given wisdom to live a wholesome, well-rounded life in relationship to God and to other people. Does God have a minutely detailed plan for every person? Friesen says, "If God's plan is thought of as a blueprint or 'dot' in the 'center of God's will' that must be discovered by the decision maker, the answer is no. On the other hand, we affirm that God does have a plan for our lives—a plan that is described in the Bible in terms that we can fully understand and apply."[3] I agree. On the whole, the Bible does not give us a prescription for finding the "center of God's will." However, it does call us into relationship with God through Christ and then challenges us to live according to what he has *already* revealed.

Think about it this way. The late English theologian John Oman said that God does not do his work like an archer firing his arrows straight into a target. Instead, God works as the rain that falls onto the mountains and then finds its way down into streams and through rivers into the oceans. The water ultimately reaches the ocean, but the trip could have been made by many routes. To apply that analogy to our lives, when we give ourselves to God through faith and prayer, God's will is ultimately achieved. In the meantime, he allows human beings to participate in its accomplishment.[4]

The traditional approach to thinking about God's

will is almost a "needle-in-a-haystack" approach. The sheer number of factors that could be involved is mind boggling. Take the idea of finding a mate, for example. Some people say that God has one person already prepared for everyone—a "Mr. Right" or a "Miss Right." But the logistics of finding that one person out of so many possibilities is overwhelming. If a person does not find that one perfect mate, does that mean he or she has sinned and is out of God's will by marrying someone else? I do not think so. Instead of only one person being a potential mate, there may be many.

To find God's will in the matter is to take seriously what the revealed will of God—the Bible—teaches us about Christian marriage. For example, we are not to be yoked with an unbeliever (2 Cor. 6:14); we are to have mutual respect for our mate (Eph. 5:21–33), and so on. More than one person will fit these criteria. Our job is to make mature, thoughtful decisions about the matter. Do I love and respect this person? Does he or she have the personal qualities that I admire and make me want to spend my life with that person? Prayer in these types of matters helps to clarify our thoughts and to center us on what is really important.

Allow me to share a personal story. My discovery of the wonder and mystery of losing myself in the life of someone else came, like many of life's good things, unexpectedly. I took a semester off from college during my second year and worked in a Christian coffeehouse across the street from the university. I had made a commitment to the Lord and had felt a "call" to ministry. At the time I had no idea what that might mean, so I took some time to explore the options.

One of the options was to attend a Christian college. I applied for admission to Louisiana College, a Baptist school in central Louisiana, and was accepted. I arrived on campus in the fall of 1971, not knowing a soul, but having more enthusiasm than I had ever known before. Several people told me that the course of study would be harder than that of the large university, and they were right. The classes were smaller, the professors got to know their students, and they expected a lot. I made many discoveries about truth, life, and myself during my first year there. One of these discoveries was that I had a mind and could use it. After all, Jesus said that we are to love God with all our minds.

That first year at Louisiana College came to a close, and I faced it with much regret. Never before had a place and a group of people become so much a part of me. But I had no money for summer school, so I had to go to work.

My brother and his wife invited me to come stay with them. He was working for a large chemical plant in Freeport, Texas, and felt sure I could get on with them. I packed a few clothes and caught a ride to their home in the little community of Oyster Creek. The day I arrived, the plant was closed by a strike!

I began scrounging around for a job—any job. School in the fall would be expensive, and there was no time to fool around. The only work I could find was selling vacuum cleaners door to door. What a predicament for a budding young theologian! I went out every day with people I did not especially like, tried to sell a product I thought was overpriced, lived in a cramped trailer with my brother and his wife, and felt more alone than I had ever felt in my life. I attended a church in Freeport several times, and each time I went I filled out the little card and checked the box, "I would like the pastor to visit me." I wanted to talk to someone, but no one from the church ever called or came by. Besides all that, I was not making much money.

A new fellow showed up at the office one day. We young salesmen were told in almost reverent tones about the selling skill of this man, so I looked forward to meeting him. I was not impressed. He and I just did not "click" at first, so I simply avoided him when I could. After all, I thought my time there was very temporary, so why take time to try to befriend someone I did not immediately like? A few months would pass and I would return to school and never see this fellow again. But "the best laid plans of mice and men . . ."

One day after work this new man invited me to our employer's house, where he and his family were staying temporarily. I showed up at the appointed time and rang the doorbell, and a girl answered. I am always suspicious of people who claim "love at first sight," but I was very impressed with her. It was not love, but it sure was interest. I learned that this girl was the daughter of the super salesman. She was my age, also a college student, and also uprooted for the summer by her family's move from Oklahoma to Texas. Had her father just "happened" to invite me over because he liked me, or could it be . . . ? I was beginning to suspect something.

As it turned out, I should have been suspicious, but I was not being set up for pain. This girl, whose name was Carla, became my friend, my confidant. We shared many interests and outlooks and began spending every spare minute together. Although both of us resisted, we felt that we were being drawn closer and closer together. After all, we had come together almost by accident, were students at schools hundreds of miles apart, and hardly had the price of a hamburger between us. How could anything possibly come of that?

My summer of isolation in Texas drew to a close, and I had mixed feelings about it. I was glad to be getting away from a job I so thoroughly disliked and looked forward to going back into an academic setting. But this girl . . .

Two people coming to love each other is a mysterious event. Logic has its place in the event, but loving is not primarily logical. My continued interest in this girl whose father had once been my boss and who lived hundreds of miles away was anything but logical. But Pascal put it so well: "The heart has its reasons that reason knows not of."

We went our separate ways that fall but ran up large phone and postage bills. Finally, toward the end of that semester, we both knew it was time to make a serious decision—end the relationship or make a commitment to each other regarding our future. With a little fear and a whole lot of youthful zeal, we decided that Carla would transfer from her university to join me at my college.

This decision changed us for the rest of our lives. We married our last semester at Louisiana College and lived on love. We had to because we did not have any money. Carla sorted letters at the post office part-time, and I was the stockman for the auto parts department at Sears. Between us we made enough to pay our $35-per-week rent on two rooms, to eat a frozen dinner each evening (which we bought three for a dollar), and to pay for books and supplies at school. Carla also worked in the cafeteria, and I tutored in the Religion Department to make a few extra dollars. Our loans and scholarships paid tuition. Most of all, we had each other. What else mattered? If that sounds like the making of a cheap novel, so be it. It is true for us, and we knew that whatever came, our commitment to each other would pull us through, and it has.

Carla and I have been married over twenty years now. We are the parents of twin teenage boys—Ryan and Christopher. How can I refer to our situation as planned, logical, or ordinary? Yet, in its own way, it is. Our story is unique in its details, but many, many people have had similar experiences of coming to love. People who did not even like each other at first later ended up "hitched." I can think of friends who are now married who met each other in a classroom—the man was the woman's high school teacher. Today they have one of the strongest families I know. Another couple began their relationship in a hospital lab, with the man as the woman's supervisor.

The point is that Carla and I had a choice in the matter. We do feel there was some providence involved, but we had to take the risk and make the choices about our lives. No one, not even God, will make your decisions for you. He certainly did not force us to marry, and we could have married someone else. The choice was ours to make.

I told the story at the beginning of chapter 4 of the young man who wanted me to pray that God would immediately send him a wife. That way of going about the business of getting a wife is clearly immature and foolish. God expects us to grow up in our faith, to make wise, mature decisions about all areas of life. J. I. Packer defines wisdom this way: "Wisdom is the power to see, and the inclination to choose, the best and the highest goal, together with the surest means of attaining it."⁵ Gaining this wisdom takes humility, work, and patience. The characteristics of biblical wisdom include reverence, humility, teachableness, diligence, uprightness, and faith. Gary Friesen writes about this wisdom as follows:

"The Christian *attitude* is to reflect, first of all, his awareness that no man, himself included, is naturally wise in himself (Prov. 3:7); and therefore, if he is to gain wisdom, it must come from some other source. Equally, his attitude must mirror his conviction that the ultimate source of wisdom is God alone. Those who refuse to acknowledge these basic realities are self-deceived fools (Rom. 1:21–22). But the posture of the one who would find wisdom is that of bowing."[6]

Wisdom is necessary to make good decisions in life. Humility and asking in prayer are necessary to gain wisdom. Prayer is necessary to gain humility and wisdom. Thus, prayer is essential to making decisions that affect our lives. Let us now consider how all of this relates specifically to finding God's will.

God's Specific Will

Finding the will of God is not nearly as difficult as some people claim. God has a general will for everyone. Paul wrote to the Ephesian Christians, "So then do not be foolish, but understand what the will of the Lord is" (5:17). Earlier he had said to them, "For I did not shrink from declaring to you the whole purpose of God" (Acts 20:27).

How did Paul know "the whole purpose of God" for the Ephesians? He knew because God's will for them is the same as it is for everyone else. For example, "The Lord is not slow about His promise, as some count slowness, but is patient toward you, not wishing for any to perish but for all to come to repentance" (2 Pet. 3:9). To young Timothy, Paul wrote, "This is good and acceptable in the sight of God our Savior, who desires all men to be saved and to come to the knowledge of the truth" (1 Tim. 2:3–4). That, on the whole, is what God wants. One theologian put it this way: "God's purpose is to create a worldwide family of persons who freely accept God as their God and who receive his love into their lives, and who respond to him by loving him with all their hearts and loving their neighbors as themselves."[7]

God wants people to be saved. Salvation comes about when people give themselves completely to God and allow him to transform them in the likeness of Christ. We learn about that desire from the Bible and from the lives of other Christians. We should be very careful about other purely subjective means of knowing something about God and his will. One scholar wrote, "Christians . . . do not behold a pillar of fire for assurance of God's presence. Nor do they consult the Urim and Thummim for His direction. Instead, they rely on the Word of God for both."[8]

God desires salvation for all people. We participate in that salvation when we accept it as God's gift, and as we pray that others might become open to it also. As we "grow up" in our faith and prayer life, we become less self-oriented and more God-oriented. Fisher Humphreys said of this orientation toward God, "Because he loves us, he will hear when we speak to him on any topic we care about. But precisely because he loves us so much, he wants us to become concerned about his 'adult' purpose. Ideally, our prayer should more and more be about achieving his purpose. We ought to be talking to him about the community, about its growth in faith and love, about the freedom of mankind, about the proclamation of the good news about Jesus."[9] We pray for God's will, which is "not an attempt to second guess God, asking for what God was going to do anyway. It is rather talking to God about achieving his purpose, and asking him to do those things which we believe will carry forward his purpose."[10]

What this means is that we will not always get our way. Prayer will not be a tool for prying out of God what he is unwilling to give. What he is willing to give is fullness in our spiritual lives (see John 10:10) and a sense of wholeness despite our circumstances. On the occasion of his eightieth birthday, John Quincy Adams said, "John Quincy Adams is well. The house in which he lives at present is dilapidated. It is tottering upon its foundation. Time and the seasons have nearly destroyed it. Its roof is pretty well worn out. Its walls are much shattered and it trembles with every wind. I think John Quincy Adams will have to move out of it soon. But he himself is well, quite well."

Those words of John Quincy Adams capture the spirit of Christians who live close to God through prayer and desiring his will. Living close to God keeps life from shrinking in on itself until the soul resembles a prune. One lady began investing in the stock market in 1944 and kept doing so until her death at age 101 in 1995. She built a portfolio worth $22 million! But she lived a loveless, shallow life.

Someone who knew her said, "A big day for her was walking down to Merrill Lynch . . . to visit her stock certificates."[11] She seems to have lived a wasted life because close relationships to others and love for God were lacking.

Making Specific Decisions

How do we make specific decisions as we seek God's will? Remember that we are not Moses, who went up the mountain and returned with the answer written in stone. We live by faith. As we pray and seek God's will in specific matters, we need to keep in mind that "God has not promised to whisper 'perfect plans' or omniscience into the mind of any believer who asks."[12]

In general, the narrow road may be wider than we think (Matt. 7:14). Many possibilities exist before us. Many choices are equally valid. As mature Christians we are to weigh the choices, apply basic principles for decision making, and make a mature choice. I realize this statement goes against what many people say they believe. They think that there is one, and only one, right choice in any matter, ranging from the clothes they wear today, to the career they have, to the person they marry. I do not believe that, on the whole, the Bible, and in particular the New Testament, supports such a concept. Strong leading by God *does* seem to occur in some circumstances, but those events seem to be the exception rather than the rule.

Gary Friesen has developed a set of principles for

decision making that I find helpful. He calls it the way of wisdom. Consider these as you prayerfully seek God's will for your life and as you make decisions.[13]

1. In areas specifically addressed by the Bible, the revealed commands and principles of God are to be obeyed. This is his moral will. For example, the Bible reveals God's will about telling the truth (Exod. 20:16). We never need to pray and ask, "Lord, should I tell the truth?" That matter is already settled. Again, the Bible reveals God's will about taking care of family (1 Tim. 5:8). The specific details of how we do that are left up to us, but the command to care for our families is not.

Some matters, then, are clearly spelled out. If we are told by the Scripture to do them, then we must do them. If we are told not to do them, we must avoid them. I mentioned earlier how I met my wife Carla. From this viewpoint, after more than twenty years of marriage, I cannot imagine my life without her. I love her dearly and consider her my best friend. But no voice from heaven told me to marry her. That was our decision to make. As it turned out, it was one of the best decisions of my life. In making that decision, we took into account our mutual devotion to Christ and our future goals.

2. In those areas where the Bible gives no command or principle (as in nonmoral decisions), the believer is free and responsible to choose his own course of action. Any decision made within the moral will of God is acceptable to God. For example, I wrote

these words on my personal laptop computer that I take with me when I travel. The Bible gives no guidance on this type of technology. Would writing this book in pencil be more spiritual or godly than using a computer? Not necessarily. It is simply not an issue dealt with in Scripture. I believe that God expects me to examine all the factors and then make a wise decision about it on my own. Since I do a great deal of writing, having a computer is much more efficient and helpful than trying to write in longhand. I actually wrote several major projects that way and can testify to the efficiency of the computer.

3. In nonmoral decisions, the objective of the Christian is to make wise decisions on the basis of spiritual expediency. After weighing all the factors involved, the right decision is one that will be the most Christ-honoring. Sometimes one choice is clearly called for, but sometimes more than one choice will fit this criterion.

For example, a young person might be considering the choices among several colleges. After examining them carefully, this student discovers they are all about the same and that any of them would offer a good education in a spiritually healthy environment. How does he choose? Does he ask God to send a sign from heaven? What God wants is children who are willing to go wherever God leads. But sometimes God lets us make the choices ourselves. In the case of the student, he needs to ask himself where he really wants to go, and then go there.

4. In all decisions, the believer should humbly submit, in advance, to the working out of God's sovereign will as it touches each decision. When Carla and I decided to marry, we trusted God with the results of our decision. In the previous example the student needs to make a choice about a college and then trust the consequences of that decision to God's sovereign purpose.

Keep in mind that even seemingly negative consequences can be the results of God's sovereignty. Not everything associated with God is soft. For example, Joe Aldrich, president of Multnomah Bible College and Seminary, was diagnosed with Parkinson's disease. Is that disease a result of sin or negligence? Could prayer remove it? Consider Aldrich's own view.

In my case I believe that Parkinson's is a custom-made instrument of grace to help me toward servanthood. Through eyes of faith I see it as a wake-up call from a loving heavenly Father. Does prayer really make a difference? Yes! I perceive that Parkinson's is an instrument that God is using to answer some of my prayers. It is deepening my confidence in God—that's an answer to prayer. It is enriching my relationship with Ruthe—that's an answer to prayer. It is broadening my understanding and my appreciation of those who are hurting—and that's an answer to prayer. It is teaching me dependence—and that's an answer to prayer. It is teaching me to pray—and that's an answer to prayer.[14]

We should be careful not to assume that if we search for God's will, we will find only happiness. God is in the process of helping people conform to the likeness of his Son. That likeness includes strengthening through trials (see 2 Cor. 4:1–17). Aldrich observed, "Most of us, it seems, don't really want God to love us—we want him to be kind to us, to mature us without pain, to teach us servanthood without serving, to develop patience without trials."

Our prayers help cause things to happen and matters to take different courses. When we pray, we work in correspondence with God's sovereignty to change our lives. This does not happen easily. Prayer is work.

Learn to take your chances with God. Pray. Prayer does not change God's ultimate will, but it allows you to lay hold of his willingness. It will not keep you from making mistakes and from taking your share of hard knocks. But prayer will bring you close to the heavenly Father who loves you more than words can describe. Ecclesiastes 9:10 reads, "Whatever your hand finds to do, do it with all your might" (NIV). That includes living and praying, and making your choices in life and then accepting the consequences. God wants the best for you. Why choose anything less?

It's Your Turn Now

- Give some thought about what you consider your life's mission.
- Do you think of that mission as God-directed?
- Write out a life-plan for the next twelve months.
- List some of the choices you face and include all of the options that seem to be viable.
- Talk to someone you consider to be spiritually mature about decisions you need to make.
- Reread all of the Scripture passages cited in this chapter.
- Develop a regular habit of praying about all of the major decisions in your life.
- Get the series of *Pray for . . .* booklets and use them as a guide for intercessory prayer for forty days. The booklets include these titles: *Pray for Your Wife* (which I wrote); *Pray for Your Husband*; *Pray for Your Pastor*; *Pray for Your Family*; and *Pray for the President*. They are available from the North American Mission Board, 4200 North Point Parkway, Alpharetta, GA 30202. Call 770–410–6000.

Questions for Further Reflection and Discussion

1. Which is more helpful as you think about finding God's will: the imagery of a target with a bull's-eye, or the imagery of rain falling on the mountain and finding its way to the ocean?

2. How do you react to the concept of making "adult" decisions? Is that a helpful suggestion?

3. Have you ever spent much time searching for God's will, only to feel like you were searching for a "needle in a haystack"?

4. What do you think is God's general will for your life?

5. Consider the statement, "The narrow road may be wider than you think." What do you think that means?

6. Gary Friesen gives four principles for decision making. Do you agree with what he said, or do you think something is lacking?

7. Consider what Joe Aldrich said he learned from his illness. Has anything in your life taught you similar things?

8. Do you think God really loves you and wants the best for you?

Endnotes

Introduction

1. Cited by Herbert Benson, M.D., with Marg Stark, *Timeless Healing: The Power and Biology of Belief* (New York: Scribner, 1996), 173.

Chapter 1

1. George Appleton, *Journey for a Soul* (Glasgow: William Collins Sons & Co., 1974), 199–200.

2. Richard B. Gardner, *Matthew*, Believers Church Bible Commentary (Scottsdale: Herald Press, 1991), 318.

3. For more on this see Don M. Aycock, *Eight Days That Changed The World* (Grand Rapids: Kregel Publications, 1997), chapter 2.

4. John Marks Templeton, *The Templeton Plan: 21 Steps to Success and Happiness*, as described to

James Ellison (San Francisco: A Giniger Book in association with Harper & Row, 1987), ix.

5. Ross Phares, *Bible in Pocket, Gun in Hand: The Story of Frontier Religion* (Lincoln: University of Nebraska Press, 1971 [1964]), 6.

6. Frederick Douglass, "Narrative of the Life of Frederick Douglass," in *The Classic Slave Narratives*, ed. Henry Louis Gates, Jr. (New York: Penguin Books USA, 1987), 286.

7. C. S. Lewis, "Does Prayer Really Change Things?" *Faith*, February–March 1989, 8.

8. *The American Heritage Dictionary of the English Language*, 1969 edition, s.v. "magic."

9. Dick Rice, quoted by Kenneth L. Woodward, "Why America Prays," *Reader's Digest*, April 1992, 200.

Chapter 2

1. Haley, quoted by Walter Anderson, *The Greatest Risk of All* (Boston: Houghton Mifflin Co., 1988), 240.

2. Donald G. Bloesch, *The Struggle of Prayer* (San Francisco: Harper & Row, 1980), 158.

3. Leon Morris, *The Gospel According to St. Luke*, Tyndale New Testament Commentaries (Grand Rapids: Eerdmans Press, 1974), 195.

4. Roosevelt, quoted by Walter Anderson, *The Greatest Risk of All* (Boston: Houghton Mifflin, 1988), 3.

5. Wilf Wilkinson, *Good News in Luke* (Glasgow: William Collins Sons, 1974), 72.

6. G. B. Caird, *Saint Luke*, The Pelican New

Testament Commentaries (Baltimore: Penguin Books, 1963), 152.

7. Herbert Benson, M.D., with Marg Stark, *Timeless Healing: The Power and Biology of Belief* (New York: Scribner, 1996), 196.

8. Ibid., 197.

9. Ibid., 300.

Chapter 3

1. Patty Roberts, *Ashes to Gold* (Waco: Word Books, 1983), 78.

2. Fisher Humphreys, *The Student*, August 1985, 27.

3. Fisher Humphreys, *The Heart of Prayer* (New Orleans: Insight Press, 1980), 89.

4. C. S. Lewis, "Does Prayer Really Change Things?" *Faith*, 1989, 9.

5. Robert H. Mounce, *Matthew, A Good News Commentary* (San Francisco: Harper & Row, 1985), 54.

6. Winston Churchill, quoted by Kenneth H. Cooper, *It's Better to Believe* (Nashville: Thomas Nelson, Inc., 1995), 31.

Chapter 4

1. Johnson, quoted by Og Mandino, *Secrets for Success and Happiness* (New York: Fawcett Columbine, 1995), 240.

2. "Hagar the Horrible," December 21, 1994.

3. Robert Coles, "The Inexplicable Prayers of

Ruby Bridges," *Christianity Today*, 9 August 1985, 19.

4. Fisher Humphreys, *The Heart of Prayer* (New Orleans: Insight Press, 1980), 55–56.

5. Ibid., 57–58.

Chapter 5

1. Lewis Grizzard, "A Miracle of Recovery Called Prayer," May 13, 1993, from his syndicated newspaper column.

2. Pascal, quoted by Og Mandino, *Secrets For Success and Happiness* (New York: Fawcett Columbine, 1995), 200.

3. Thoreau, quoted by Mandino, ibid., unnumbered preface page.

4. Charles H. Rabon, "Be Still and Know—An Experiment in Prayer," *Quarterly Review*, January–March, 1988, 35.

5. This letter is from Bruce Larsen, *Dare to Live Now* (Grand Rapids: Zondervan, 1965), 83.

Chapter 6

1. James Leo Green, *Jeremiah*, The Broadman Bible Commentary, vol. 6 (Nashville: Broadman Press, 1971), 81.

2. Ibid., 110.

3. C. S. Lewis, "Does Prayer Really Change Things?" in *Faith*, February–March, 1989, 8.

4. Elizabeth Achtemeier, *Jeremiah*, Knox Preaching Guides (Atlanta: John Knox Press, 1987), 64.

Chapter 7

1. Curtis C. Mitchell, "Why Keep Bothering God?" *Christianity Today*, 13 December 1985, 34.

2. P. T. Forsyth, quoted by Mitchell, ibid., 34.

3. For more on this night in Jesus' life, see my book *Eight Days That Changed the World* (Grand Rapids: Kregel Publications, 1997). This book examines the last week of Jesus' life, from Palm Sunday to Easter Sunday.

4. These findings are from Dr. Herbert Benson, *The Relaxation Response*, and are well summarized by Dr. Kenneth Cooper in *It's Better to Believe* (Nashville: Thomas Nelson, Inc., 1995), 28. See another of Benson's books, *Timeless Healing: The Power of Biology and Belief*, with Marg Stark (New York: Scribner, 1996).

5. Cooper, *It's Better to Believe*, ibid., 28.

Chapter 8

1. Gary Friesen, with J. Robin Maxson, *Decision Making and the Will of God: A Biblical Alternative to the Traditional Approach* (Portland: Multnomah Press, 1980), 182. (Italics mine.)

2. Ibid., 86.

3. Ibid., 113.

4. For further discussion on this, see Fisher Humphreys, *The Heart of Prayer* (New Orleans: Insight Press, 1980), 54–55.

5. Packer, quoted by Friesen, 188.

6. Friesen, 193.

7. Humphreys, 89.

8. Friesen, 245.

9. Humphreys, 92.

10. Ibid., 93.

11. See the cover story in *Money*, January 1996.

12. Friesen, 261.

13. Ibid., 257.

14. Joe C. Aldrich, "When Bad News Comes," *Decision*, April 1996, 32–33.

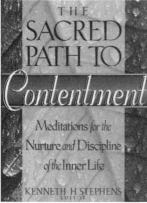
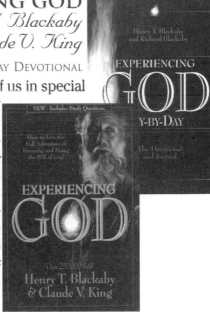